Adopt AI or Get *Replaced*

Future belongs to those who adapt today.

AYUSH SHARMA

COPYRIGHT

First Edition: May 2026

Printed in the India

www.victorusai.com

"To those who refuse to be left behind in the age of AI."

Keep learning.

Keep adapting.

Keep building the future.

"The greatest danger in times of turbulence is not the turbulence -- it is to act with yesterday's logic."

-- Peter Drucker

"The illiterate of the 21st century will not be those who cannot read and write, but those who cannot learn, unlearn, and relearn."

-- Alvin Toffler

"The best way to predict the future is to create it."

-- Abraham Lincoln

A Message from the Author

When I set out to write this book, I had one goal: to give you a clear, honest, and practical guide to navigating the most significant technological shift of our lifetime. Not a book full of hype. Not a book designed to scare you. A book that actually helps.

I wrote Adopt AI or Get Replaced because I watched too many intelligent, capable people fall behind -- not because they lacked talent or work ethic, but because they were waiting. Waiting for AI to settle down. Waiting until they felt ready. Waiting for someone to give them permission to begin.

This book is that permission.

The strategies in these pages are practical and immediately applicable. The case studies are drawn from real patterns of transformation I have observed across industries. The 30-day action plan at the end of this book was designed so that you can start making meaningful progress today -- not someday.

You do not need a technology background. You do not need to be young. You do not need to abandon your current career. You simply need a willingness to learn and the courage to begin.

The future belongs to those who adapt today. I genuinely believe that -- and I wrote every chapter of this book with the conviction that you are fully capable of becoming one of those people.

Thank you for trusting me to be part of your journey.

Acknowledgements

A book is never the work of one person, even when a single name appears on the cover. This one is no exception.

To the readers who will hold this book and take its lessons seriously: you are the reason it was worth writing. Every example, every framework, every case study was crafted with you in mind. Thank you for trusting these pages with your time.

To the countless professionals, students, freelancers, and entrepreneurs whose stories -- shared in communities, conversations, and classrooms -- inspired the case studies in this book: your courage to adapt and share what you learned made this work richer than I could have made it alone.

To the teams behind ChatGPT, Claude, Midjourney, Notion, Canva, and Grammarly: thank you for building technology that genuinely empowers people. The tools you have created are changing lives.

To my family and friends who supported this project with patience and encouragement through long writing sessions and late nights: your belief in this work carried me through the moments when the blank page felt impossible.

To my mentors, teachers, and the communities that shaped how I think about technology, learning, and human potential -- this book reflects your influence on every page.

And finally, to everyone who has ever felt left behind by technological change: this book is for you. The future is not closed. It is wide open -- and it is yours to claim.

TABLE OF CONTENTS

Preface

Artificial intelligence has arrived -- not with the dramatic fanfare of science fiction, but quietly, practically, and with profound implications for every person who works, creates, learns, or leads. In the span of just two years, AI went from a topic discussed mostly in academic papers to a tool used by hundreds of millions of people around the world.

And yet, most people are still on the sidelines.

Some are waiting. Some are skeptical. Some are overwhelmed. Some genuinely do not know where to start. This book exists for all of them.

Adopt AI or Get Replaced is not a technical manual. It is not a research paper. It is a practical guide -- written in plain English, built on real examples, and structured around what actually works for real people in real situations.

The title is blunt because the reality is blunt. AI is not going away. It is not a trend. It is a fundamental shift in how work gets done, how value is created, and how careers are built. The people who understand this and act on it will have an extraordinary advantage. The people who do not will find themselves increasingly left behind -- not because they are less talented, but because they chose not to adapt.

This book will show you how to adapt. It will show you what AI actually is, how it works in plain terms, which tools are worth your time, and how to use them effectively. It will give you a concrete, day-by-day action plan to start your own transformation.

That goal is achievable. For anyone. Starting today.

Introduction

Let me start with a question: What separates the people who thrive in a period of technological change from the people who struggle?

It is not intelligence. It is not credentials. It is not even experience.

It is timing and willingness. The willingness to learn something unfamiliar. The willingness to experiment, fail, adjust, and try again. And the timing to start before everyone else does.

Right now, in 2025, we are at one of those rare inflection points in history. AI has crossed from the domain of specialists into the hands of everyone. You do not need a technical background, a large budget, or years of experience. You need curiosity and a willingness to start.

This book is organized to take you from zero to capable in a logical sequence. Here is what you will find in each chapter:

- Chapter 1 explains what AI actually is, without jargon or hype.
- Chapter 2 examines the real impact of AI on jobs and skills -- not catastrophizing headlines, but the nuanced reality of what is changing.
- Chapter 3 introduces the essential AI tools you should know, with step-by-step setup instructions.
- Chapter 4 teaches you prompt engineering -- the single most important skill for getting great results from AI.

- Chapter 5 shows you how to boost your productivity in email, research, writing, and content creation.
- Chapter 6 helps you future-proof your career and position yourself for higher pay.
- Chapter 7 brings everything to life through detailed case studies of people who transformed their situations using AI.
- Chapter 8 gives you a complete, day-by-day 30-day action plan to put everything into practice immediately.

Read this book with a device nearby. Try the tools as you encounter them. Do not just read -- do. Now, let us begin.

CHAPTER

01

Understanding the AI Revolution

CHAPTER

The AI Revolution is Here

Let me ask you something: When was the last time you went a full day without using something powered by artificial intelligence? If you're thinking, "Wait, I don't use AI"—think again. Did you unlock your phone with your face today? That's AI. Did you ask Siri or Google Assistant a question? AI. Did you scroll through TikTok, Instagram, or YouTube and notice how eerily well the algorithm knows what you want to watch? Yep, that's AI too. Did Netflix recommend a show you ended up binge-watching? AI again. Here's the thing: AI isn't coming. It's already here. It's in your pocket, on your screen, and woven into nearly every app and service you use daily. But here's what most people don't realize—and what this book is really about—AI isn't just something happening to you. It's something you can use for you. And the people who figure that out? They're about to have an unfair advantage.

The Speed of Change is Breathtaking

In November 2022, a company called OpenAI released a tool called ChatGPT. Within five days, it had one million users. Within two months, it had 100 million users—making it the fastest-growing consumer application in history. Faster than Instagram. Faster than TikTok. Faster than anything that came before it. Why? Because for the first time, regular people—not just programmers or tech experts—could have a conversation with AI and get genuinely useful answers. Students used it to understand complex topics. Writers used it to brainstorm ideas. Freelancers used it to draft emails, create content, and solve problems faster than ever before. But here's where it gets interesting: while millions of people were experimenting with ChatGPT, millions of others dismissed it. "It's just a fad." "It makes mistakes." "I don't need that." "I'll wait and see." Fast forward to today. The people who started using AI early? Many of them have already transformed how they work. They're finishing projects in half the time. They're learning new skills faster. They're getting promoted, landing better clients, and building careers that didn't exist two years ago. The people who waited? They're starting to feel the gap. I'm not telling you this to make you panic. I'm telling you this because there's still time—but the window is closing fast. The AI revolution isn't something that's going to happen in ten years. It's happening right now, and the decisions you make in the next few months will determine whether you ride the wave or get left behind.

The Stakes Are Personal

Let's get real for a second. You're reading this book because you sense something is changing. Maybe you've heard people talking about AI at work or school. Maybe you've seen job postings that mention "AI skills preferred." Maybe you've watched someone in your field start using AI and suddenly become way more productive than everyone else. Or maybe you're just tired of feeling like technology is moving faster than you can keep up. Here's what I want you to understand: The future won't be decided by your degree, your years of experience, or even how smart you are. It will be decided by how effectively you can use AI. That might sound dramatic, but it's true. Think about it this way: Thirty years ago, being "computer literate" was a nice bonus. Today, if you can't use a computer, you're essentially unemployable in most fields. AI is following the same path—except it's happening ten times faster. The good news? You don't need to become a programmer. You don't need a computer science degree. You don't even need to understand how AI works under the hood. You just need to learn how to use it effectively—and that's exactly what this book will teach you.

Why This Matters for YOU (Yes, You)

Maybe you're a student trying to figure out what career path makes sense in a world where AI is changing everything. Maybe you're a freelancer competing with people who are using AI to work faster and cheaper. Maybe you're a young professional watching your company adopt AI tools and wondering if your job is safe. Here's the truth: AI is not your enemy. It's your opportunity. The people who will thrive in the next decade aren't the ones who resist AI or fear it.

They're the ones who learn to work with it. They're the ones who use AI to amplify their creativity, accelerate their learning, and multiply their productivity. Think of AI as a superpower that's available to everyone—but only if you're willing to learn how to use it. Let me give you an example.

Sarah is a 24-year-old graphic designer. A year ago, she was spending hours creating social media graphics for clients, manually resizing images, writing captions, and brainstorming ideas. Then she started using AI tools. Now, she uses ChatGPT to generate caption ideas in seconds, Midjourney to create unique visual concepts, and AI-powered design tools to automate repetitive tasks. Her output tripled. Her income doubled. And she's working fewer hours than before. Or take Marcus, a 19-year-old college student studying marketing. He used to spend entire weekends researching for papers and struggling to organize his thoughts. Now he uses AI to help him research faster, outline his ideas, and even catch grammar mistakes. He's getting better grades and has more time for internships—which, by the way, he landed partly because he could talk intelligently about AI in his interviews. These aren't tech geniuses. They're regular people who decided to stop waiting and start learning.

The Myth That's Holding You Back

Here's the biggest lie people tell themselves about AI: "It's too complicated for me." Let me be blunt: that's nonsense. Using AI today is easier than learning to use Instagram was ten years ago. You don't need to code. You don't need to understand algorithms. You don't need a tech background. You just need to be willing to try. Think about it: You learned how to use Google, right? You type in a question, and it gives you answers. Using AI tools like ChatGPT is basically the same thing—except instead of getting a list of links, you get direct answers, ideas, and solutions. The people who are "good at AI" aren't smarter than you. They just started earlier. And the beautiful thing about starting now? You're still early. AI is so new that most people—including most professionals in your field—are still figuring it out. If you start today, you can catch up and even get ahead faster than you think.

What This Chapter Will Do for You

By the end of this chapter, you're going to understand three critical things:

1. What AI actually is —in plain English, without the jargon or hype

2. Why the myths about AI are wrong —and why you're more capable of using it than you think

3. Why starting now matters —and what's at stake if you don't

This isn't about scaring you. It's about empowering you. Because once you understand what AI really is and how accessible it actually is, you'll realize something important: You're not behind. You're right on time. Let's get started.

What AI Actually Is (Without the Jargon)

Alright, let's clear something up right away: When most people hear "artificial intelligence," they picture robots, sci-fi movies, or some mysterious technology that only graduates can understand.

Forget all that. AI, at its core, is actually pretty simple. It's just software that can learn from examples and make decisions or predictions based on what it's learned. That's it. Let me give you an analogy. Remember when you were learning to ride a bike? At first, you wobbled and fell. But after enough practice, your brain figured out how to balance without you consciously thinking about it. AI works similarly—except instead of learning to balance a bike, it learns to recognize patterns, answer questions, generate text, create images, or make recommendations. The reason AI feels so powerful right now is that we've finally reached a point where AI can learn from massive amounts of information—like, the entire internet—and use that knowledge to do useful things for regular people.

The Three Types of AI You'll Actually Use

You don't need to become an AI expert, but understanding three basic concepts will make everything else in this book make sense. Don't worry—I'll keep it simple.

1. Machine Learning (The Foundation) Machine learning is the backbone of modern AI. Here's how it works in the simplest terms possible: Imagine you're teaching a kid to recognize dogs. You show them hundreds of pictures of dogs—big dogs, small dogs, fluffy dogs, short-haired dogs. Eventually, the kid's brain learns what makes something a "dog," even if they've never seen that specific breed before. Machine learning works the same way. You feed a computer thousand (or millions) of examples, and it learns to recognize patterns. That's how your phone learns to recognize your face, how Spotify knows what music you'll like, and how your email filters out spam. You don't need to know how to build machine learning systems. You just need to know that when you're using AI tools, there's a system in the background that learned from tons of examples and is now applying that knowledge to help you.

2. Large Language Models (The Conversational AI) This is the technology behind tools like ChatGPT, Claude, and Google's Bard. These are AI systems that have been trained on enormous amounts of text from the internet—books, articles, websites, conversations—and learned how language works. Think of a large language model (or LLM) as someone who's read almost everything ever written and can now have a conversation with you about almost any topic. It can write, explain, summarize, brainstorm, translate, code, and more—all through simple conversation. Here's what makes LLMs so powerful: You don't need to learn a special programming language or click through complicated menus. You just talk to them like you'd talk to a knowledgeable friend. You ask a question, give an instruction, or describe what you need—and the AI responds. For example:

- "Explain quantum physics like I'm ten years old."
- "Write a professional email declining a job offer."
- "Give me five creative ideas for a birthday party."
- "Help me outline an essay about climate change."

The AI understands what you're asking and generates a response based on everything it's learned. It's not perfect—it makes mistakes sometimes—but it's shockingly good at understanding context and providing useful answers.

3. Prompts (How You Talk to AI) Here's the secret that separates people who get amazing results from AI and people who get mediocre results: how you ask matters. A "prompt" is simply the instruction or question you give to an AI. The clearer and more specific your prompt, the better the AI's response will be. Think of it like ordering food at a restaurant. If you say, "I want food," the waiter won't know what to bring you. But if you say, "I'd like the grilled salmon with steamed vegetables and a side salad, dressing

on the side," you'll get exactly what you want. AI works the same way. Compare these two prompts: Vague prompt: "Write something about marketing." Specific prompt: "Write a 200-word Instagram caption for a small coffee shop promoting a new seasonal latte. Use a friendly, warm tone and include a call-to-action encouraging people to visit this weekend." The second prompt will get you a much better result because you've given the AI context, specifics, and clear expectations. Don't worry—you'll get really good at writing prompts as you practice. In fact, "prompt engineering" (which is just a fancy term for "knowing how to ask AI for what you want") is becoming one of the most valuable skills you can have. We'll dive deep into this in Chapter 4.

How AI Actually Works (The 30-Second Version)

You don't need to understand the technical details, but here's the basic idea:

1. Training: AI systems are "trained" by feeding them massive amounts of data (text, images, videos, etc.). During training, the AI learns patterns—like which words usually go together, what makes an image look like a cat versus a dog, or how to solve certain types of problems.

2. Inference: Once trained, the AI can take new information (like your question or prompt) and use what it learned to generate a response, make a prediction, or complete a task.

3. Iteration: The more you use AI and refine your prompts, the better your results get. It's a conversation, not a one-time command. That's it. You don't need to know the math, the code, or the algorithms. You just need to know that AI learns from examples and then applies that learning to help you.

Why Understanding This Matters

Here's why I'm taking the time to explain this: When you understand what AI actually is, it stops feeling like magic or something intimidating. It becomes a tool—a really powerful tool that you can learn to use. You don't need to know how a car engine works to drive a car. You don't need to know how the internet works to browse websites. And you don't need to know how neural networks function to use AI effectively. But having a basic understanding helps you:

- Ask better questions (write better prompts)
- Know what AI can and can't do (so you don't waste time on impossible tasks)
- Feel confident experimenting (because you understand the basics)

Think of this section as your foundation. Now that you know what AI is in simple terms, you're ready to start using it. And trust me—once you start, you'll wonder how you ever worked without it.

The Myths vs. The Reality

Let's talk about the elephant in the room—or rather, the six elephants. There are a bunch of myths floating around about AI, and they're stopping people from taking action. Maybe you've heard some of these. Maybe you've even believed them. I don't blame you—the media loves to sensationalize AI, and it's hard to know what's true and what's hype. So let's bust these myths right now. Because the sooner you see through them, the sooner you can start using AI to your advantage.

Myth #1: "AI Will Replace Me and Everyone I Know"

The Reality: AI won't replace you. But someone using AI might. Let's get this straight: Yes, AI is automating certain tasks. Yes, some jobs will change or disappear. But here's what the fear-mongers don't tell you: AI is a tool, not a replacement for human creativity, judgment, and connection. Think about what happened when calculators were invented. Did they replace mathematicians? No. They freed mathematicians from tedious calculations so they could focus on solving bigger, more complex problems. AI is doing the same thing across every industry. Here's the truth: AI is really good at repetitive, predictable tasks—data entry, basic research, generating first drafts, scheduling, and so on. But it's terrible at things that require human judgment, emotional intelligence, creativity, and strategic thinking. A graphic designer who uses AI to generate concepts faster isn't being replaced—they're becoming more valuable because they can deliver more ideas in less time. A writer who uses AI to research and outline isn't obsolete—they're more productive and can take on more clients. The people who will struggle aren't the ones being "replaced by AI." They're the ones refusing to learn how to use it. What you should do: Stop fearing AI and start learning how to use it as your assistant. The goal isn't to compete with AI—it's to collaborate with it.

Myth #2: "I Need to Be a Programmer or Tech Genius to Use AI"

The Reality: If you can use Google, you can use AI. This might be the most damaging myth of all because it stops people from even trying. Here's the truth: Modern AI tools are designed for regular people. You don't need to write code. You don't need to understand algorithms. You don't need a computer science degree. Using ChatGPT is literally as simple as typing a question into a text box. Using AI image generators like Midjourney or DALL-E is as simple as describing what you want to see. Using AI tools for productivity, writing, or research is often easier than using traditional software. Let me give you a real example. My friend Jessica is a 28-year-old event planner. She barely knows how to use Excel. But she uses ChatGPT every single day to draft emails, brainstorm event themes, create checklists, and even write social media posts for her clients. She didn't take a course. She didn't read a manual. She just started typing questions and experimenting. That's it. That's the barrier to entry. What you should do: Stop waiting to "learn enough" before you start. Just open ChatGPT (it's free) and start asking it questions. You'll figure it out in five minutes.

Myth #3: "AI Is Only for Big Tech Companies"

The Reality: AI is more accessible now than ever before—and it's often free. A few years ago, this myth was actually true. AI required expensive infrastructure, specialized teams, and massive budgets. Only companies like Google, Amazon, and Facebook could afford to build and use AI at scale. But that's changed completely. Today, you can access some of the most powerful AI tools in the world for free or for a few bucks a month. ChatGPT has a free version. Google's Bard is free. Canva has AI features built in. Grammarly uses AI to improve your writing. Notion has AI assistants. The list goes on. Freelancers, students, small business owners, and solo creators are using the exact same AI technology that billion-dollar companies use. The playing field has been leveled in a way that's never happened before in tech. What you should do: Take advantage of this moment. You have access to tools that would have cost millions of dollars just a few years ago. Use them.

Myth #4: "AI Is Dangerous and Will Take Over"

The Reality: AI is a tool, not a sentient being plotting world domination. Okay, let's address the sci-fi fear. Yes, there are legitimate conversations happening among researchers about AI safety and ethics. Yes, we should be thoughtful about how AI is developed and used. But no, ChatGPT is not going to become self-aware and enslave humanity. The AI you'll be using in this book—and in your daily life—is narrow AI. That means it's designed to do specific tasks, like answer questions, generate text, or create images. It doesn't have consciousness, desires, or intentions. It's software. Very sophisticated software, but software nonetheless. Think of it like a car. Cars are powerful and can be dangerous if misused. But we don't avoid learning to drive because cars exist. We learn to use them safely and responsibly. The same applies to AI. Are there risks? Sure—misinformation, bias in AI systems, privacy concerns. But those are problems we solve by being informed and thoughtful users, not by avoiding AI altogether. What you should do: Use AI responsibly. Fact-check important information. Don't blindly trust everything AI tells you. But don't let fear stop you from learning a tool that can genuinely improve your life.

Myth #5: "I'll Never Catch Up—It's Too late to Start"

The Reality: You're not late. You're early. This is the myth that breaks my heart the most because it's so completely wrong. Here's the truth: AI as we know it today—conversational AI that regular people can use—has only been mainstream for about two years. TWO YEARS. We're still in the early innings of this game. Most people in your field, your school, or your industry are still figuring this out. Most companies are still experimenting. Most professionals are still learning. You're not behind—you're right on time. And here's the beautiful part: Because AI is so new, you can catch up incredibly fast. Unlike learning a traditional skill that takes years to master, you can become proficient with AI tools in weeks or even days. Think about it this way: If you started learning AI today and spent just 30 minutes a day practicing, you'd be ahead of 90% of people within a month. That's not an exaggeration. Most people are still in the "I'll get to it eventually" phase. If you start now, you'll have a massive head start. What you should do: Stop thinking you're behind and start thinking you're early. The best time to start was yesterday. The second-best time is right now.

Myth #6: "It's Too Complicated for Me"

The Reality: AI tools are designed to be simple—often simpler than the tools you already use. Let me ask you something: Do you use social media? Do you use Google? Do you use apps on your phone? If you answered yes to any of those, you're already using interfaces that are more complicated than most AI tools. The beauty of modern AI is that it's conversational. You don't need to learn keyboard shortcuts, navigate complex menus, or memorize commands. You just talk to it. You describe what you want. You ask questions. The AI figures out the rest. Compare that to learning something like Photoshop or Excel, which have hundreds of features, buttons, and functions you need to memorize. AI is actually easier because it meets you where you are. Here's a real example: My cousin David is 19 and not particularly "tech-savvy." He struggled with Microsoft Word. But he uses ChatGPT every day to help him study, write essays, and even plan his schedule. Why? Because talking to ChatGPT feels natural. He doesn't have to learn anything complicated—he just asks it questions like he'd ask a friend. What you should do: Give yourself permission to be a beginner. Start with simple tasks. Ask basic questions. You'll be shocked at how quickly it clicks.

Your AI Journey Starts Here

Let's take a breath and recap what we've covered in this chapter. First , you learned that the AI revolution isn't coming—it's already here. It's in your phone, your apps, and increasingly, your workplace. The people who learn to use AI now will have a massive advantage over those who wait.

Second, you learned what AI actually is, without the jargon. It's not magic or rocket science. It's software that learns from examples and helps you get things done faster and better. You don't need to be a programmer or a tech genius to use it—you just need to be willing to try.

Third, you busted the myths that might have been holding you back. AI won't replace you (but someone using AI might). It's not too complicated. It's not too late. And it's not just for tech companies or experts. It's for you. Here's what I want you to take away from this chapter: AI is accessible. AI is learnable. And your future depends on starting now—not on mastering it overnight, but on simply beginning. You don't need to become an AI expert. You don't need to understand every technical detail. You just need to be willing to experiment, make mistakes, and learn as you go. Think of this book as your guide. Over the next seven chapters, I'm going to show you exactly how to use AI to boost your productivity, learn faster, work smarter, and future-proof your career. We'll cover the essential tools, the skills you need, real-world examples, and a step-by-step action plan to get you started. But here's the thing: None of that matters if you don't believe you can do this. So let me be clear: You can do this. You're not too old, too young, too inexperienced, or too "non-technical." You're exactly where you need to be. And if you commit to learning AI—even just a little bit each day—you'll be amazed at how quickly you progress. The AI revolution is here. The question isn't whether it's going to change your life—it's whether you're going to be the one in control of that change. Let's make sure the answer is yes. In the next chapter, we're going to dive into how AI is transforming jobs and skills right now—and more importantly, what that means for you and your career. You'll see exactly where the opportunities are, what skills matter most, and how to position yourself to thrive in this new landscape. But before we move on, I want you to do one thing: Open ChatGPT (or any AI tool) and ask it one simple question. Anything. "What's the weather today?" "Give me a recipe for chocolate chip cookies." "Explain photosynthesis in simple terms." Just try it. Get comfortable with the idea that you can have a conversation with AI. That's step one. Because once you take that first step, everything else becomes possible. Let's go.

CHAPTER

02

AI's Impact on Jobs and Skills

CHAPTER

The Day Everything Changed

Let me tell you about Emma. Emma is 26 years old. She's a marketing coordinator at a mid-sized tech company. For three years, she's been doing what marketing coordinators do: writing blog posts, creating social media content, drafting email campaigns, analyzing performance metrics, and coordinating with designers. She's good at her job. She gets positive reviews. She works hard. Then, six months ago, her company started using AI tools. At first, Emma was skeptical. She watched as her colleague Jake started using ChatGPT to draft blog posts in minutes instead of hours. She saw the design team using Midjourney to generate concept images instantly. She noticed the sales team using AI to personalize hundreds of emails at once. Emma kept doing things the old way. "I don't need AI," she thought. "My work is creative. It requires a human touch." But here's what happened: Jake started producing three times as much content—and it was good. The design team was churning out more concepts in a day than they used to in a week. The sales team's email response rates doubled. Meanwhile, Emma was still spending two hours writing a single blog post. Still manually creating social media graphics one by one. Still doing everything the way she'd always done it. Three months later, Jake got promoted. Emma didn't. Here's the thing: Emma isn't lazy. She isn't incompetent. She's just competing in a new game with old rules. And in this new game, the people who use AI aren't just a little bit ahead—they're exponentially ahead. This isn't a story about Emma losing her job. It's a story about Emma losing ground. And it's happening to millions of people right now, in every industry, in every country. The question isn't whether AI will change your job. It already is. The question is: Are you going to be like Jake, or are you going to be like Emma? Let's talk about what's really happening out there.

How AI Is Transforming Jobs

RIGHT NOW

Forget the predictions and the think pieces about what might happen in ten years. Let's talk about what's happening today, in real companies, to real people. AI isn't coming for your job in some distant future. It's already reshaping how work gets done. And the transformation is happening faster than most people realize. Here's what you need to understand: AI isn't replacing entire jobs (yet). It's replacing tasks within jobs. And the people who figure out how to use AI to handle the boring, repetitive tasks are freeing themselves up to do the high-value, creative, strategic work that actually matters. Let's break down what's happening in specific fields. I'm going to show you exactly what's being automated, what's becoming more valuable, and what this means for anyone working in these areas.

Marketing and Content Creation: The Productivity Explosion

If you work in marketing, content creation, or anything related to writing and design, you're in the eye of the storm right now. What's Being Automated:

- First drafts of blog posts, articles, and social media captions Basic graphic design and image creation
- Email copywriting and personalization at scale
- SEO keyword research and content optimization Ad copy variations and A/B testing
- Social media scheduling and basic analytics What's Becoming MORE Valuable
- Strategic thinking: What message will resonate? What story should we tell?
- Brand voice and authenticity: Making AI-generated content sound human and on-brand
- Creative direction: Guiding AI to produce the right concepts

- Audience understanding: Knowing what your audience actually wants
- Editing and refinement: Taking AI's 80% solution and making it 100%

Here's a real example: A freelance copywriter I know named Marcus used to charge $500 for a landing page and spend 4-5 hours writing it. Now he uses ChatGPT to generate multiple drafts in 20 minutes, then spends 2 hours refining, personalizing, and perfecting them. He still charges $500 (sometimes more, because his quality is better), but he can now take on three times as many clients. His income tripled in six months. The copywriters who are struggling? They're the ones still writing everything from scratch, taking 5 hours per project, and wondering why clients are going elsewhere. The Bottom Line: If you're in marketing or content creation and you're not using AI, you're competing with one hand tied behind your back. But if you learn to use AI as your assistant—to handle the grunt work while you focus on strategy and creativity—you become unstoppable.

Software Development: Coding at the Speed of Thought

If you thought programming was safe from AI, think again. AI is transforming software development faster than almost any other field. What's Being Automated:

- Writing boilerplate code and repetitive functions
- Debugging and error detection
  Code documentation and comments
- Converting code between programming languages

- Writing unit tests
- Searching documentation and Stack Overflow

(AI just knows the answers now) What's Becoming MORE Valuable:

- System design and architecture: Understanding how pieces fit together
- Problem-solving: Defining what needs to be built and why
- Code review and quality assurance: Knowing what good code looks like
- Domain expertise: Understanding the business problem you're solving
- Collaboration and communication: Working with non-technical stakeholders

Here's what's happening: Tools like GitHub Copilot, ChatGPT, and Claude can now write functional code from simple descriptions. A developer can say, "Write a function that takes a list of users and returns only those who signed up in the last 30 days," and the AI will generate working code in seconds. Does this mean developers are obsolete? Absolutely not. But it means the job is changing. Junior developers who used to spend days writing basic CRUD operations can now generate that code in minutes and focus on learning system design. Senior developers who used to spend hours debugging can now identify issues instantly and spend their time on architecture and optimization. A developer friend of mine, Priya, told me this: "I used to spend 60% of my time writing code and 40% thinking about problems. Now I spend 20% writing code and 80% thinking. And I'm building better software than ever." The Bottom Line: Developers who resist AI will find themselves outpaced by developers who embrace it. But developers who learn to use AI as a coding partner—to handle the tedious parts while they focus on design and problem-solving—will be more productive and valuable than ever.

Data Analysis and Business Intelligence: From Spreadsheets to Insights

If your job involves working with data—analyzing it, visualizing it, or making decisions based on it—AI is about to become your best friend or your worst nightmare, depending on how you respond. What's Being Automated:

- Data cleaning and preparation
  Basic statistical analysis
- Creating charts and visualizations
- Writing SQL queries
  Generating reports and summaries
- Identifying patterns and anomalies in datasets
  What's Becoming MORE Valuable:
- Asking the right questions: What should we be measuring and why?
- Business context: Understanding what the data actually, means for the company
- Strategic recommendations: Turning insights into action
- Data storytelling: Communicating findings to

non-technical audiences

- Critical thinking: Knowing when the data is

misleading or incomplete Here's the shift: AI can now analyze a dataset and tell you what's happening. But it can't tell you why it matters or what to do about it. That's where humans come in. Let me give you an example. A business analyst named Kevin used to spend three days every month pulling data, cleaning it, creating pivot tables, and generating reports. Now he uses AI tools to do all of that in about two hours. What does he do with the extra time? He spends it talking to department heads, understanding their challenges, and using data to solve real business problems. His manager told him, "You've become ten times more valuable this year." Why? Because Kevin stopped being a report generator and became a strategic advisor. The Bottom Line: If your value is in manipulating spreadsheets, you're in trouble. But if your value is in understanding what the numbers mean and what to do about them, AI just made you incredibly powerful.

Customer Service and Support: The Human Touch Amplified

Customer service is being transformed by AI, but not in the way most people think. What's Being Automated:

- Answering common questions (FAQs, order status, basic troubleshooting)
- Routing tickets to the right department
  Generating response templates
- Translating conversations in real-time
- Analyzing customer sentiment

Following up on resolved issues

What's Becoming MORE Valuable:

- Empathy and emotional intelligence: Handling upset or frustrated customers Complex problem-solving: Dealing with unique or unusual situations
- Relationship building: Turning customers into advocates
- Escalation judgment: Knowing when to involve a human

Product feedback: Identifying patterns and communicating them to the product team Here's what's happening in customer service: AI chatbots are handling 60-80% of routine inquiries. That sounds scary if you're a customer service rep, right? But here's the twist: The companies that are doing this well aren't firing their customer service teams. They're redeploying them to handle the complex, high-value interactions that AI can't manage. A customer service manager named Lisa told me this: "We used to have 20 people answering the same questions over and over. Now we have AI handling those, and our team of 15 focuses on the customers who really need help—the ones with complicated issues, the ones who are upset, the ones who need a human touch. Our customer satisfaction scores have never been higher, and our team is way less burned out." The Bottom Line: If your job is answering the same questions all day, AI is coming for that. But if you're good at solving complex problems and making customers, feel heard, you're about to become more valuable than ever.

Administrative and Knowledge Work:

The Efficiency Revolution

This is the big one. If your job involves emails, scheduling, data entry, research, document creation, or any kind of "knowledge work," AI is changing everything. What's Being Automated:

- Email drafting and responses
- Meeting scheduling and calendar management
  Data entry and form filling
- Document summarization
- Research and information gathering
  Transcription and note-taking
- Expense reporting and basic bookkeeping
  What's Becoming MORE Valuable:
- Judgment and decision-making: Choosing the right course of action
- Relationship management: Building and maintaining professional connections
- Strategic planning: Thinking ahead and anticipating needs
- Communication skills: Conveying complex ideas clearly
  Project management: Coordinating people and resources
  Here's a real-world example: An executive assistant named Rachel used to spend 15 hours a week on email management, scheduling, and meeting prep. Now she uses AI to draft emails, suggest meeting times, and summarize documents. She spends maybe 5 hours a week on those tasks. What does she do with

the extra 10 hours? She's become a strategic partner to her executive—anticipating needs, managing relationships, and handling high-level coordination. Her salary increased by 40% this year. Meanwhile, administrative workers who are still doing everything manually are finding their roles being eliminated or consolidated. The Bottom Line: If your value is in doing tasks, you're vulnerable. But if your value is in thinking, deciding, and managing relationships, AI just freed you up to do more of what actually matters.

The Skills That Are Disappearing (And Which Ones Matter More)

Let's be honest about what's happening: Some skills that used to be valuable are becoming less valuable. And some skills that used to be "nice to have" are becoming essential. This isn't about being mean or pessimistic. It's about being realistic so you can adapt.

The Skills Losing Value

Here's what's becoming less valuable in the age of AI:

1. Repetitive, Rule-Based Tasks If your skill is following a process—data entry, basic bookkeeping, simple coding tasks, form filling—AI can do it faster and more accurately. These skills aren't worthless yet, but they're worth less every month.

2. Basic Information Retrieval Remember when being good at Google was a skill? Or knowing where to find information in a manual? AI can now search, synthesize, and summarize information instantly. Just knowing where to find things isn't enough anymore.

3. First-Draft Creation Whether it's writing, design, or code, AI can now generate decent first drafts. If your entire value proposition is "I can create a first draft," you're in trouble. The value has shifted to refinement, strategy, and creative direction.

4. Memorization and Recall AI has perfect memory and instant recall. If your skill is remembering facts, procedures, or information, that's no longer a competitive advantage.

5. Basic Translation and Transcription AI can translate between languages and transcribe audio with near-perfect accuracy. If that's your primary skill, you need to add more value on top of it. Here's the hard truth: If a task can be described by a clear set of rules or steps, AI can probably do it—or will be able to soon. But before you panic, let's talk about what's becoming MORE valuable.

The Skills Gaining Value

While some skills are declining in value, others are skyrocketing. And here's the good news: These are often the more interesting, creative, and human skills.

1. Critical Thinking and Judgment AI can give you options, but it can't tell you which option is right for your specific situation. The ability to evaluate information, consider context, and make sound decisions is more valuable than ever. Example: AI can generate five different marketing strategies. But knowing which one will actually work for your brand, your audience, and your budget? That's human judgment.

2. Creativity and Innovation AI can remix and recombine existing ideas, but it struggles with truly original thinking. The ability

to come up with novel solutions, creative concepts, and innovative approaches is increasingly valuable. Example: AI can design a logo based on your description. But coming up with a brand identity that captures the essence of a company and resonates with customers? That's human creativity.

3. Emotional Intelligence and Empathy AI can't read a room. It can't sense when someone is upset, build genuine relationships, or navigate complex social dynamics. These human skills are becoming more valuable as AI handles the technical stuff. Example: AI can draft a response to a customer complaint. But knowing when to break the rules, offer a personal touch, or escalate to save a relationship? That's emotional intelligence.

4. Strategic Thinking AI is great at tactics but struggles with strategy. The ability to see the big picture, anticipate future trends, and make long-term plans is more valuable than ever. Example: AI can optimize your ad campaigns. But deciding whether you should be running ads at all, or if you should pivot your entire marketing strategy? That's strategic thinking.

5. Domain Expertise AI has broad knowledge but lacks deep expertise in specific fields. If you have deep knowledge of an industry, a craft, or a specialized area, you can use AI to amplify that expertise in ways that generalists can't. Example: AI can write about healthcare. But a doctor using AI to research, draft patient communications, and stay current with medical literature? That's domain expertise amplified by AI.

6. AI Literacy and Collaboration And here's the new essential skill: knowing how to work with AI effectively. This is the skill that separates people who thrive from people who struggle. Think of it

this way: Twenty years ago, being "computer literate" meant you could use email and Word. Today, if you can't use a computer, you're essentially unemployable in most fields. AI literacy is following the same path—except it's happening ten times faster.

The New Baseline: AI as a Fundamental Skill

Here's what you need to understand: AI literacy is becoming a baseline skill, not a specialized skill. In five years, saying "I know how to use AI" will be like saying "I know how to use email" today. It won't make you special—but not knowing how will make you unemployable. The people who will thrive aren't the ones who are "good at AI" in some technical sense. They're the ones who can combine AI with their existing skills to become exponentially more effective.

- A writer who uses AI becomes a content machine
- A designer who uses AI becomes a creative powerhouse
- A developer who uses AI becomes a building machine
- An analyst who uses AI becomes a strategic advisor
- A marketer who uses AI becomes a growth engine The pattern is clear: AI doesn't replace human skills. It amplifies them. But only if you learn to use it.

Your Choice: Two Paths Ahead

Let's cut through the noise and talk about what this really means for you. You're standing at a fork in the road. One path leads to growth, opportunity, and relevance. The other leads to stagnation, struggle, and obsolescence. The choice is yours. But you need to understand what each path looks like.

Path 1: Adapt and Thrive

Let's talk about what happens when you choose to embrace AI and learn to use it effectively. You'll Complete Work Faster and Better This is the most immediate benefit. When you use AI to handle the repetitive, time-consuming parts of your work, you free up time for the high-value stuff. Remember Marcus, the copywriter? He's not working harder—he's working smarter. He's using AI to generate drafts, research topics, and create variations. Then he applies his expertise to refine, personalize, and perfect the work. Result: He's producing three times as much work in the same amount of time. And because he has more time to focus on quality, his work is actually better than before. You'll Earn More Here's a simple equation: If you can produce more value in less time, you can either work less or earn more. Most people choose to earn more. Freelancers who adopt AI can take on more clients. Employees who adopt AI become more valuable and get promoted faster. Entrepreneurs who adopt AI can scale their businesses without hiring more people. A graphic designer I know named Tanya used to make $50,000 a year. After learning to use AI tools like

Midjourney and ChatGPT, she tripled her output and raised her rates. She now makes $120,000 a year and works fewer hours. You'll Stay Relevant and Competitive This is the big one. In a world where AI is becoming standard, the people who know how to use it will have a massive advantage over those who don't. Think about it: If you're competing for a job or a client against someone who can work three times faster than you because they use AI, who's going to win? The job market is already shifting. More and more job postings mention "AI skills" or "experience with AI tools." Companies are actively looking for people who can use AI to drive results. If you start learning now, you'll be ahead of 90% of people in your field within six months. You'll Have More Interesting, Creative Work Here's something people don't talk about enough: AI doesn't just make you more productive—it makes your work more interesting. When AI handles the boring, repetitive stuff, you get to focus on the creative, strategic, meaningful work. You get to spend more time thinking, creating, and solving interesting problems. Rachel, the executive assistant I mentioned earlier, told me this: "I used to spend my days drowning in emails and scheduling. Now I spend my days thinking strategically and solving real problems. My job is so much more interesting now." That's the promise of AI: not just more productivity, but more meaningful work.

Path 2: Ignore It and Fall Behind

Now let's talk about what happens if you choose to ignore AI or wait to see what happens. You'll Compete with People Who Have an Unfair Advantage This is already happening. In every field, there are people using AI to work faster, produce more, and deliver better results. If you're not using AI, you're competing with one hand tied behind your back. You're the person still writing everything by hand while everyone else is using a word processor. And here's the thing: Your clients, your boss, and your colleagues won't care that you're doing things "the old way." They'll just notice that you're slower and less productive than everyone else. Your Work Will Become Less Valuable As AI becomes more common, the baseline for what's expected will rise. Work that used to take a week will be expected in a day. Quality that used to be "good enough" will become the minimum standard. If you're not using AI to keep up with these rising expectations, your work will seem slow, outdated, and less valuable. You'll Miss Opportunities Jobs, promotions, clients, projects—they're all going to people who can demonstrate AI skills and productivity. I've talked to hiring managers who told me they're actively filtering out candidates who don't mention AI skills. I've talked to freelancers who lost clients to competitors who could deliver faster using AI. I've talked to employees who got passed over for promotions because their colleagues were more productive. The opportunities are going to people who adapt. If you don't, you'll watch them pass you by. You'll Risk Becoming Obsolete This is the harsh reality: In five years, not knowing how to use AI will be like not knowing how to use email today. It will be a disqualifying factor. The people who refuse to learn AI won't just be at a disadvantage—they'll be unemployable in many fields. I'm not saying this to scare you. I'm saying it because it's true, and you need to understand the stakes.

The Choice Is Yours—But the Window Is Closing

Here's the thing about these two paths: Right now, you can still choose which one you take. But the window for making that choice is closing. AI is moving fast. The people who start learning now will have a massive head start over the people who wait. And the people who wait too long will find themselves so far behind that catching up feels impossible. But here's the good news: You're not too late. Not even close. Most people are still in the "wait and see" phase. Most professionals in your field are still figuring this out. Most companies are still in the early stages of AI adoption. If you start today—right now—you can catch up and get ahead faster than you think.

What This Means for YOU

Let's make this personal. I don't know exactly what you do for a living. Maybe you're a student trying to figure out your career path. Maybe you're a freelancer trying to stay competitive. Maybe you're a young professional trying to advance in your company. But here's what I do know: AI is going to impact your work, your career, and your earning potential—whether you're ready for it or not. The question isn't whether AI will change your field. It will. The question is whether you're going to be the person who uses that change to your advantage or the person who gets left behind by it.

How to Think About Your Own Situation

Here's what I want you to do right now: Think about your current job or the career you're pursuing. Ask yourself these questions: 1. What tasks do I do that are repetitive or rule-based? These are the tasks that AI can probably automate or assist with. Identify them. These are your opportunities to use AI to free up time. 2. What tasks do I do that require judgment, creativity, or human connection? These are the tasks where you add unique value. These are the tasks you should be spending more time on. AI can help you get there by handling the other stuff. 3. What would I do with an extra 10 hours a week? If AI could handle the boring parts of your job, what would you do with the time you save? Learn new skills? Take on more clients? Focus on strategy? That's your opportunity. 4. Who in my field is already using AI? Look around. Who's getting ahead? Who's more productive? Chances are, they're using AI. Study what they're doing. Learn from them. 5. What's the cost of waiting? Be honest with yourself. If you wait six months, a year, two years to start learning AI, what will you miss out on? What opportunities will pass you by?

The Reality Check

Let me be straight with you: Learning AI isn't optional anymore. It's not a "nice to have" skill. It's not something you can put off until later. It's the difference between thriving and struggling in the next decade. But here's the good news: It's not as hard as you think. And you don't need to become an expert overnight. You don't need to understand how AI works under the hood. You don't need to learn to code. You don't need a computer science degree. You just need to start using AI tools, experimenting with them, and learning how to apply them to your work. And that's exactly what the rest of this book is going to teach you.

Your Advantage: You're Still Early

Here's something that should make you feel better: Despite everything I've said about AI transforming jobs, most people still aren't using it effectively. Most professionals are still in the "I've heard of ChatGPT but haven't really tried it" phase. Most companies are still figuring out their AI strategy. Most industries are still in the early stages of adoption. That means if you start now—today—you can get ahead of the curve. You can be the person in your company, your field, or your network who "gets" AI. You can be the one who helps others learn. You can be the one who positions themselves as forward-thinking and adaptable. The early adopters are winning right now. And you can still be an early adopter if you start today.

What Comes Next

In the next chapter, we're going to get practical. I'm going to introduce you to the essential AI tools that every beginner needs to know. We'll talk about what they do, how to use them, and how to get started—even if you've never used AI before. But before we get there, I need you to make a decision. Are you going to be like Emma—watching from the sidelines while others get ahead? Or are you going to be like Jake, Marcus, Priya, Kevin, Lisa, and Rachel—people who saw the change coming and decided to ride the wave instead of fighting it? The choice is yours. But you need to choose.

The Transformation Isn't Coming. It's Here.

Let me leave you with this: A year ago, most people thought AI was science fiction or something only tech companies cared about. Today, AI is in your phone, your apps, and increasingly, your workplace. Six months from now, AI will be even more integrated into how work gets done. A year from now, it will be standard. Two years from now, not knowing how to use AI will be a serious disadvantage. The transformation isn't coming. It's happening right now, in real time, in every industry. The people who recognize this and take action will thrive. The people who wait will struggle. But here's the good news—the news I want you to hold

onto as we move forward: You still have time. You can still get ahead. And it's easier than you think. You don't need to become an AI expert. You don't need to change careers. You don't need to start over. You just need to start learning. Start experimenting. Start using AI as your assistant, your collaborator, your productivity multiplier. And that journey starts in the next chapter. We're going to talk about the AI tools you actually need to know—the ones that will make an immediate difference in your work and your life. We're going to cut through the hype and focus on what's practical, accessible, and useful. No more theory. No more "what if." Just practical, actionable steps you can take today. Are you ready? Let's go.

CHAPTER

03

Essential AI Tools for Beginners

CHAPTER

Why Tool Knowledge Matters

Let me ask you something: Have you ever walked into a gym for the first time and felt completely lost? You see all these machines. Treadmills, weight racks, cable systems, rowing machines. Everyone around you seems to know exactly what they're doing. They walk up to equipment, adjust settings, and get to work. Meanwhile, you're standing there thinking, Where do I even start? Here's the thing: those people aren't necessarily smarter or more talented than you. They just know which equipment does what. They know that the treadmill is for cardio, the bench press builds chest strength, and the rowing machine works your whole body. Once you know what each tool does, the gym stops being intimidating. It becomes a place where you can actually get results. AI tools work the same way. Right now, there are hundreds—maybe thousands—of AI tools out there. New ones launch every week. Some are incredible. Some are overhyped. Some are free. Some cost money. And if you're just starting out, it's easy to feel overwhelmed by the sheer number of options. But here's what I want you to understand: knowing which tools exist and what they're good for is literally half the battle. You don't need to master every AI tool on the planet. You don't need a computer science degree. You don't even need to understand how the technology works under the hood. You just need to know which tools solve which problems—and how to access them. Think of it like this: everyone has access to the same gym equipment, but the person who knows where to go and what to use gets results faster. The same is true with AI. The tools are available to everyone. The advantage goes to the people who know which ones to use and when. That's what this chapter is about. I'm going to walk you through the essential AI tools that every beginner should know. These aren't obscure, complicated platforms that require a PhD to operate. These are accessible, user-friendly tools that you can start using today—most of them for free. By the end of this chapter, you'll have a clear understanding of:

- Which AI tools are worth your time (and which ones you can ignore for now) How to set up and start using each one
- Real examples of how people like you are already using these tools to get ahead
- A simple checklist to get your AI toolkit up and running this week You're not going to be overwhelmed. You're going to be equipped. Let's get you armed with the right toolkit.

ChatGPT: Your First AI Assistant

This is where everything starts. If you're going to use one AI tool—just one—it should be ChatGPT. I'm serious. If you walked away from this chapter right now and only set up ChatGPT, you'd still be miles ahead of most people. It's that powerful. It's that versatile. And it's shockingly easy to use. So, what is ChatGPT? In the simplest terms, it's a conversational AI. You type something in, and it responds. Like texting a really smart friend who knows a little bit about everything. You can ask it questions, give it tasks, brainstorm ideas, get feedback, learn new concepts—basically anything you'd use Google for, but with the added benefit of having a back-and-forth conversation. Here's what makes it different from a search engine: Google gives you links. ChatGPT gives you answers. Google makes you dig through ten articles to find what you need. ChatGPT synthesizes information and hands it to you in plain language. Let me give you a real example. Meet Priya, a 22-year-old college student studying biology. She's taking a physics class (required, not her favorite), and she's completely lost on the concept of quantum mechanics. She's read the textbook three times. She's watched YouTube videos. Nothing is clicking. One night, frustrated and desperate, she opens ChatGPT and types: "Explain quantum mechanics to me like I'm 10 years old." Thirty seconds later, ChatGPT responds with an explanation involving marbles, magic tricks, and how particles can be in two places at once. For the first time all semester, Priya actually understands what her professor has been talking about. She didn't need to watch another hour-long lecture. She didn't need to hire a tutor. She just needed someone—or something—to explain it in a way that made sense to her. That's the power of ChatGPT.

How to Get Started (It's Easier Than You Think)

Alright, let's get you set up. I'm going to walk you through this step-by-step, and I promise it's going to feel ridiculously simple.

Step 1: Go to chat.openai.com That's it. Just type that into your browser. You'll land on the ChatGPT homepage.

Step 2: Sign up for a free account Click "Sign up." You can use your email, or you can sign in with your Google or Microsoft account (which is even faster). Enter your info, verify your email, and you're in. Total time: about 90 seconds.

Step 3: Choose your plan Here's where you have a decision to make: free or paid? The free version of ChatGPT (called GPT-3.5) is incredibly powerful. It can write essays, answer questions, help you brainstorm, debug code, summarize articles—basically everything you need to get started. Most beginners should start here. The paid version (ChatGPT Plus, $20/month) gives you access to GPT-4, which is smarter, faster, and more accurate. It also gives you priority access during peak times (so you're not waiting in a queue) and access to plugins and advanced features like DALL-E image generation. My recommendation? Start with the free version. Use it for a week or two. If you find yourself using it every single day and wishing it were faster or more powerful, upgrade. But don't feel pressured to pay right away. The free version is more than enough to see real results.

Step 4: Explore the interface Once you're in, you'll see a simple screen. There's a text box at the bottom where you type your message. That's it. No complicated menus. No settings to configure. Just a blank canvas waiting for you to ask it something. On the left side, you'll see your chat history. Every conversation you have gets saved there, so you can come back to it later. At the top, there's a button to start a new chat. Use this when you want to switch topics or start fresh. That's the whole interface. Seriously. If you can send a text message, you can use ChatGPT.

Let's Try Something Right Now

I want you to do this with me. Open ChatGPT (or imagine you're doing it if you're reading this on the go), and let's run a quick experiment. Type this into the chat box: "I'm a [your profession or field of study]. Give me 5 ways I can use AI to work faster and smarter." Hit enter. Watch what happens. Within seconds, ChatGPT will generate a personalized list of ideas tailored to your field. If you're a student, it might suggest using AI to summarize research papers or generate study guides. If you're a freelance writer, it might recommend using AI to brainstorm article ideas or draft outlines. If you're in marketing, it might suggest automating social media captions or analyzing competitor strategies. This is your first taste of what's possible. You didn't need to read a manual. You didn't need to watch a tutorial. You just asked a question, and it gave you a useful answer. Now try this: "Explain [a concept you've been struggling with] in simple terms." Maybe it's a work concept, a school topic, or something you've been curious about but never fully understood. Type it in. See what happens. You're going to be shocked at how easy this is.

Real Example: The Student Who Stopped Struggling

Let me tell you about Marcus, a 19-year-old computer science student. Marcus was drowning in assignments. Between coding projects, math homework, and essays for his general education classes, he was pulling all-nighters just to keep up. He felt like he was always behind, always scrambling, always stressed. Then a friend told him about ChatGPT. At first, Marcus was skeptical. How is a chatbot going to help me with coding? But he decided to try it anyway. He started small. When he got stuck on a Python assignment, instead of spending an hour Googling error message, he pasted his code into ChatGPT and asked, "Why isn't this working?" ChatGPT didn't just tell him the answer. It explained the logic, pointed out the mistake, and suggested a fix. Marcus understood it immediately. Then he tried something else. He had an essay due for his philosophy class—a subject he hated. He asked ChatGPT to help him brainstorm arguments for his thesis. Within minutes, he had a structured outline and three solid points to build his essay around. By the end of the semester, Marcus wasn't pulling all-nighters anymore. He was finishing assignments in half the time. His grades improved. His stress levels dropped. And he finally had time to actually enjoy college. Here's what Marcus told me: "I used to think asking for help was cheating. Now I realize it's just working smarter. ChatGPT doesn't do the work for me—it helps me understand it faster." That's the mindset shift I want you to have.

What You Can Actually Do With ChatGPT

Let's get specific. Here are some of the most common ways people use ChatGPT: For students:

- Explain difficult concepts in simple language
- Generate study guides and flashcards
- Brainstorm essay topics and outlines

- Summarize long research papers
- Practice for exams with custom quizzes

For freelancers and professionals: Draft emails, proposals, and reports

- Brainstorm project ideas
- Edit and improve your writing Research competitors or industry trends
- Automate repetitive writing tasks

For creatives:

- Generate blog post ideas
- Write social media captions
- Develop character backstories for fiction
- Brainstorm marketing campaigns
- Overcome writer's block

For anyone:

- Learn new skills (ask it to teach you something step-by-step)
- Plan your day or week
- Get advice on tough decisions
- Translate languages
- Have a conversation when you need to think out loud The point is this: ChatGPT isn't just one tool. It's a Swiss Army knife. The more you use it, the more uses you'll discover.

This Single Tool Is a Game-Changer

I'm not exaggerating when I say that ChatGPT alone can transform how you work, study, and create. You don't need to master it overnight. You don't need to become an expert. You just need to start using it. Open it up. Ask it a question. See what happens. Experiment. Play around. Get comfortable with the idea that you now have a tool that can help you think faster, work smarter, and learn more efficiently. This is your starting point. Everything else builds from here.

Image Generation Tools: Midjourney & DALL-E

If ChatGPT is your writing assistant, these are your creative visual partners. Let me paint a picture for you (pun intended): You're working on a presentation. You need a custom image—something specific, something unique. Maybe it's a futuristic cityscape for a business pitch. Maybe it's an illustration of a concept for a school project. Maybe it's a logo idea for your side hustle. In the old world, you had three options:

1. Spend hours searching stock photo sites and settling for something "close enough"

2. Hire a designer and wait days (or weeks) for a result

3. Try to make it yourself in Photoshop and end up with something that looks... not great In the new world?

You describe what you want in a sentence, and AI generates it in 30 seconds. Welcome to the world of AI image generation.

What Are DALL-E and Midjourney?

These are tools that create images from text descriptions. You type what you want to see, and the AI generates it. No design skills required. No software to learn. Just words. Let's break down the two most popular options: DALL-E (made by OpenAI, the same company behind ChatGPT) is integrated directly into ChatGPT if you have the paid version. It's user-friendly, accessible, and great for beginners. You can generate images right inside your ChatGPT conversations, which makes it incredibly convenient. Midjourney is a standalone tool that runs through Discord (a messaging app). It's known for producing higher-quality, more artistic images. The learning curve is slightly steeper, but the results are often stunning. Both are powerful. Both are worth knowing about. And both are easier to use than you think.

Who Actually Uses These Tools?

Let me give you some real-world examples: Students use them to create visuals for presentations, posters, and projects. Instead of spending hours searching for the perfect image, they generate exactly what they need in minutes. Designers use them to speed up the ideation process. Instead of sketching dozens of concepts by hand, they generate variations instantly and refine the ones that work. Content creators use them to produce eye-catching graphics for social media, blog posts, and YouTube thumbnails. Custom visuals that would have cost hundreds of dollars to commission are now generated on demand. Entrepreneurs use them to create logos, product mock-ups, and marketing materials without hiring a designer. The common thread? These tools don't replace creativity. They amplify it.

Real Example: The Designer Who Tripled Her Output

Meet Aisha, a 26-year-old freelance graphic designer. Aisha loved her work, but she was constantly stressed about deadlines. Every client project required hours of brainstorming, sketching, and revising. She could only take on a few clients at a time because each project took so long. Then she discovered Midjourney. At first, she was skeptical. Won't this make me obsolete? But she decided to experiment. She started using Midjourney to generate initial concepts for client projects. Instead of spending two hours sketching ideas, she'd spend 20 minutes generating dozens of variations with AI. Here's what happened: her process went from two hours of concept development to 30 minutes. She could present clients with more options, faster. And because she was generating ideas so quickly, she had more time to focus on the refinement and customization that clients actually valued. Within three months, Aisha had tripled her client load. She was earning more, working less, and delivering better results. Her secret? She didn't let AI replace her skills. She used it to handle the grunt work so she could focus on the creative decisions that actually mattered.

How to Get Started With DALL-E

If you already have ChatGPT Plus (the $20/month version), you already have access to DALL-E. Here's how to use it: Step 1: Open ChatGPT and start a new chat. Step 2: Type a description of the image you want. Be specific. Instead of "a dog," try "a golden retriever puppy sitting in a field of sunflowers at sunset, photorealistic style." Step 3: Hit enter and wait about 10-15 seconds. Step 4: ChatGPT will generate an image based on your description. If you don't love it, you can ask it to modify it: "Make the sunset more orange" or "Add mountains in the background." That's it. You just created a custom image without touching a design program. If you're on the free version of ChatGPT, you won't have access to DALL-E yet. But you can sign up for a free trial of DALL-E directly at labs.openai.com. You'll get a handful of free credits to experiment with.

How to Get Started With Midjourney

Midjourney requires a few extra steps, but it's still beginner-friendly. Step 1: Download Discord (it's free) if you don't already have it. It's available on desktop and mobile. Step 2: Go to midjourney.com and click "Join the Beta." This will add the Midjourney bot to your Discord account. Step 3: Open Discord and find the Midjourney server in your server list. Step 4: Go to one of the "newbies" channels (they're designed for beginners). Step 5: Type /imagine followed by your image description. For example: /imagine a futuristic city at night with neon lights and flying cars Step 6: Wait about 60 seconds. Midjourney will generate four variations of your image. Step 7: If you like one of them, you can upscale it (make it higher resolution) or create more variations. Midjourney gives you a limited number of free image generations to start. After that, it's $10/month for the basic plan. But those free credits are enough to get a feel for how it works.

Understanding Prompts: The Key to Great Images

Here's the thing about AI image generation: the quality of your output depends entirely on the quality of your input. If you type "a cat," you'll get... a cat. Generic. Boring. Forgettable. But if you type "a fluffy white cat with blue eyes sitting on a windowsill, soft morning light, watercolour painting style," you'll get something beautiful and specific. The more detail you provide, the better the result. Here are some tips for writing great image prompts: Be specific about the subject: Instead of "a person," say "a young woman with curly hair wearing a red jacket." Describe the setting: "in a coffee shop," "on a mountain peak," "in a futuristic laboratory." Specify the style: "photorealistic," "oil painting," "cartoon style," "minimalist line art." Include lighting and mood: "soft golden hour light," "dramatic shadows," "bright and cheerful." Add details: "with mountains in the background," "holding a book," "surrounded by flowers." The more you practice, the better you'll get at describing exactly what you want.

Common Misconception: "I'm Not Artistic Enough"

I hear this all the time: "I'm not creative. I can't even draw a stick figure. How am I supposed to use these tools?" Here's the truth: you don't need to be artistic to use AI image generation. You just need to be able to describe what you want. Think about it this way: if you can order food at a restaurant, you can use DALL-E or Midjourney. You're not cooking the meal—you're just telling the chef what you want. The AI handles the execution. You handle the vision. And here's the beautiful part: the more you use these tools, the more your creative confidence grows. You start to see possibilities you never noticed before. You start to think visually. You start to experiment. You don't need to be an artist. You just need to be curious.

You Just Described What You Want, and It Made It Real

Let that sink in for a second. You typed a sentence. The AI generated an image. No design degree. No expensive software. No hours of work. This is the world we live in now. And if you're thinking, This feels like magic — you're right. It kind of does. But it's not magic. It's just technology that's finally caught up to what we've always wanted: the ability to bring our ideas to life without needing years of training. So go ahead. Open DALL-E or Midjourney. Describe something you've always wanted to see. Watch it appear in front of you. You're not just consuming content anymore. You're creating it.

Productivity & Organization Tools: Notion, Canva, Grammarly

Not everything needs ChatGPT. Don't get me wrong—ChatGPT is incredible. But it's not the only AI tool you should know about. There are other platforms that integrate AI into tools you might already be using (or should be using). These tools don't replace ChatGPT; they complement it. Think of it this way: ChatGPT is your general-purpose assistant. These other tools are specialists. They're designed to solve specific problems—organization, design, writing polish—and they do it really, really well. Let's talk about three of the most useful ones: Notion AI, Canva AI, and Grammarly.

Notion AI: Your Research and Organization Powerhouse

If you've never heard of Notion, here's the quick version: it's an all-in-one workspace where you can take notes, organize projects, build databases, and collaborate with others. Think of it as a combination of Google Docs, Trello, and Evernote, all in one place. Now add AI to that, and you've got Notion AI. Here's what makes it powerful: Notion AI can help you synthesize information, organize scattered notes, and turn messy thoughts into structured documents. It's like having a personal assistant who's really good at making sense of chaos. Real-world use cases: For students: Let's say you're writing a research paper. You've got notes from ten different sources scattered across multiple documents. Notion AI can summarize those notes, pull out key themes, and help you organize them into a coherent outline. What used to take hours now takes 20 minutes. For freelancers: You're managing multiple client projects, each with its own deadlines, deliverables, and notes. Notion AI can help you create project templates, generate status updates, and even draft client emails based on your notes. For anyone: You've got a messy brain dump of ideas. Notion AI can turn that into a structured to-do list, a project plan, or a blog post outline. Here's a real example: Emma, a 23-year-old graduate student, was drowning in research for her thesis. She had hundreds of pages of notes, articles, and excerpts, but no clear way to organize them. She was spending more time searching for information she'd already found than actually writing. Then she started using Notion AI. She dumped all her notes into Notion, and the AI helped her categorize them by theme, summarize key points, and generate an outline for each chapter of her thesis. What used to take her an entire weekend now took two hours. Emma told me: "I finally feel like I'm in control of my research instead of drowning in it." How to get started:

- Go to notion.so and sign up for a free account
- Explore the templates (there are tons for students, freelancers, and professionals)
- Try the AI features (you get a limited number of free AI responses; after that, it's $10/month)
- Start with something simple: ask Notion AI to summarize a long document or generate a to-do list from your notes

Canva AI: Design Without the Design Skills

Canva is a design platform that's been around for years. It's known for being beginner-friendly—you don't need Photoshop skills to create professional-looking graphics. Now, with Canva AI, it's even easier. Here's what Canva AI can do:

- Generate design templates based on your description Write copy for social media posts, flyers, and presentations
- Remove backgrounds from images instantly
- Suggest colour schemes and layouts
- Resize designs for different platforms

(Instagram, Facebook, LinkedIn, etc.) with one click Real-world use cases: For content creators: You need to create five Instagram posts for the week. Instead of staring at a blank canvas, you tell Canva AI what you want, and it generates templates. You tweak the colors and text, and you're done. Total time: 20 minutes instead of two hours. For students: You're making a presentation for class. Canva AI suggests layouts, generates slide content based on your topic, and even recommends images. You go from blank slides to a polished deck in under an hour. For small business owners: You need a flyer for an event. Canva AI generates multiple design options based on your event details. You pick the one you like, make a few tweaks, and you're ready to print. Here's a real example: Jake, a 28-year-old freelance social media manager, was managing five clients. Each client needed custom graphics every week—posts, stories, ads. He was spending 10+ hours a week just on design. Then he started using Canva AI. Instead of designing each post from scratch, he'd describe what he needed, and Canva would generate templates. He'd customize them with the client's branding, and he was done. His design time dropped from 10 hours a week to 3. Jake told me: "I used to dread design day. Now it's the easiest part of my week." How to get started:

- Go to canva.com and sign up for a free account

Explore the templates (there are thousands for every use case)

- Try the AI features: Magic Write (generates text),

Background Remover, Magic Resize Start with something simple: create a social media post or a presentation slide

Grammarly AI: Beyond Grammar

You've probably heard of Grammarly. It's the tool that catches your typos and grammar mistakes. But Grammarly has evolved. It's not just a grammar checker anymore—it's an AI-powered writing assistant. Here's what modern Grammarly can do:

- Detect tone (does your email sound too harsh? too casual?)

- Suggest clarity improvements (is your sentence too wordy or confusing?)
- Offer style recommendations (make your writing more confident, more friendly, more professional)
- Generate text based on prompts (similar to ChatGPT, but integrated into your writing)

Real-world use cases: For students: You're writing an essay, and you're not sure if your argument is clear. Grammarly highlights confusing sentences and suggests simpler alternatives. For professionals: You're writing an email to your boss, and you want to sound confident but not aggressive. Grammarly analyzes your tone and suggests adjustments. For freelancers: You're drafting a proposal for a client. Grammarly catches not just typos, but also weak phrasing and unclear explanations. Here's a real example: Liam, a 24-year-old marketing coordinator, was constantly second-guessing his emails. He'd write a message, delete it, rewrite it, and still feel unsure. He was spending 20 minutes on emails that should have taken 5. Then he started using Grammarly. The AI would flag sentences that sounded too passive or too aggressive. It would suggest stronger word choices. It would even tell him if his tone didn't match his intent. Liam told me: "I finally feel like I sound like myself—just a more polished version." How to get started:

- Go to grammarly.com and sign up for a free account
- Install the browser extension (it works in Gmail, Google Docs, LinkedIn, and most websites)
- Start writing. Grammarly will automatically suggest improvements as you type.
- Try the free version first; upgrade to Premium ($12/month) if you want advanced tone and style suggestions

How These Tools Work Together

Here's the beautiful part: these tools aren't isolated. They work together to create a seamless workflow. Let me show you what I mean: Scenario: You're creating a blog post.

1. You brainstorm ideas and outline your post in Notion AI

2. You write the first draft in Notion or Google Docs with Grammarly checking your grammar and tone as you type

3. You ask ChatGPT to suggest a catchy headline and meta description

4. You create a featured image for the post using DALL-E or Midjourney

5. You design social media graphics to promote the post using Canva AI

Total time: 2-3 hours instead of a full day. Scenario: You're preparing for a presentation.

1. You organize your research notes in Notion AI and generate an outline

2. You create your slides in Canva, using AI-generated templates and copy

3. You write your speaker notes in Google Docs with Grammarly ensuring clarity

4. You use ChatGPT to practice answering potential questions Total time: 3-4 hours instead of a full weekend. See how they fit together? Each tool handles a specific part of the process, and

together they create a workflow that's faster, smoother, and less stressful.

These Fit Seamlessly Into Tools You're Already Using

Here's what I want you to understand: you don't need to overhaul your entire workflow to start using AI. You don't need to abandon Google Docs or Microsoft Word. You don't need to stop using the tools you're comfortable with. These AI tools integrate into your existing process. Grammarly works inside Gmail and Google Docs. Canva connects to your social media accounts. Notion syncs with your calendar and task manager. You're not learning a whole new system. You're just adding a layer of intelligence to what you're already doing. And that's the point. AI isn't about replacing your workflow—it's about making it better.

Free vs. Paid: Making Smart Choices

Let's talk about money. By now, you've probably noticed that some of these tools are free, some have free versions with limitations, and some require a subscription. And if you're a student, a freelancer just starting out, or someone on a tight budget, you might be wondering: Do I really need to pay for these tools? Short answer: Not right away. Let me give you a framework for making smart decisions about when to use free tools and when it's worth investing in paid versions.

Start Free, Upgrade When You Feel the Ceiling

Here's my philosophy: start with free versions, and only upgrade when you're actively frustrated by the limitations. Most AI tools offer generous free tiers that are more than enough for beginners. You can accomplish a lot without spending a dime. The free versions are designed to let you explore, experiment, and figure out which tools you actually use. Only upgrade when you hit a wall. When you find yourself thinking, I wish this were faster, or I need more features, or I'm using this every single day — that's when you consider paying. Don't upgrade because you think you're supposed to. Upgrade because the tool has proven its value to you.

The Budget-Conscious Approach

Let's be real: if you're a student or early in your career, you probably don't have a lot of extra cash lying around. And that's okay. You don't need premium versions of every tool to see results. Here's a realistic free-tool starter pack: ChatGPT (Free version): Incredibly powerful. You can do 90% of what you need without paying. Notion (Free version): Generous free tier with unlimited pages and basic AI features. Canva (Free version): Thousands of templates and basic design features. You won't have access to premium templates or advanced AI features, but you can still create professional-looking graphics. Grammarly (Free version): Catches grammar and spelling mistakes. You won't get tone detection or advanced style suggestions, but it's still useful. DALL-E (Free trial): You get a handful of free image generations to experiment with. With just these free tools, you can:

- Write better, faster
- Organize your work and research
- Create professional designs
- Generate custom images
- Automate repetitive tasks

That's a complete AI toolkit without spending a cent.

When Does It Make Sense to Pay?

Now, let's talk about when upgrading is worth it. Here's a simple ROI (return on investment) calculation: If a tool saves you time, how much is that time worth? Let's say ChatGPT Plus costs $20/month. If it saves you 5 hours a week, that's 20 hours a month. If your time is worth even $10/hour (whether that's freelance income, study time, or just personal time you value), then you're getting $200 worth of value for $20. That's a 10x return. Here's another way to think about it: If a tool helps you earn more money, it pays for itself. Let's say you're a freelance writer. Canva Pro costs $13/month. If it helps you create better portfolio pieces or social media content that lands you one extra client worth $500, it's paid for itself 38 times over. Or let's say you're a student. Notion AI costs $10/month. If it helps you organize your research and write papers faster, and that extra time lets you take on a part-time gig that earns you $100/month, it's paid for itself 10 times over. The math is simple: if the tool creates more value than it costs, it's worth it.

Real Math: How Much Do You Need to Earn Extra to Justify It?

Let's get specific. Here are the most common paid upgrades and what you'd need to earn (or save in time) to justify them: ChatGPT Plus ($20/month):

- If you're a freelancer earning $25/hour, you need to save 48 minutes per month to break even If you're a student and your time is worth $15/hour, you need to save 80 minutes per month Canva Pro ($13/month):
- If you create content for clients or your own business, you need to earn an extra $13/month from better-looking designs If you're a student, you need to save about 50 minutes per month (at $15/hour) Notion AI ($10/month):
- If you're a professional earning $30/hour, you need to save 20 minutes per month If you're a student, you need to save about 40 minutes per month Grammarly Premium ($12/month):
- If you write professionally, you need to save about 30 minutes per month (at $25/hour) If you're a student, you need to save about 48 minutes per month See the pattern? These tools don't need to save you hours every day to be worth it. They just need to save you a little bit of time consistently—or help you produce better work that leads to better opportunities.

You Don't Need to Spend Money to Start

Here's what I want you to take away from this section: you don't need to spend money to start using AI. The free versions are powerful. They're enough to see real results. They're enough to build new skills, boost your productivity, and get ahead of your peers. Start free. Experiment. Figure out which tools you actually use. Then, when you're ready—when you're actively frustrated by the limitations or when you can clearly see the ROI—upgrade. Don't feel pressured to pay for tools you're not using. Don't feel like you're missing out if you stick with free versions. You're not behind. You're being smart.

Start Free, Upgrade When You're Ready

That's the strategy. Simple, practical, and budget-friendly. You're not trying to buy your way to success. You're trying to use the right tools at the right time. And right now, the right move is to start with free tools and see what happens.

Your AI Toolkit Setup Checklist

Alright, we've covered a lot. You now know about ChatGPT, DALL-E, Midjourney, Notion AI, Canva, and Grammarly. You understand what they do, how to use them, and when it makes sense to pay for premium versions. But here's the thing: knowledge without action is just trivia. You can read about these tools all day, but until you actually set them up and start using them, nothing changes. So let's turn this knowledge into action. I'm going to give you a simple, actionable checklist. These are the 7 things you should do this week to get your AI toolkit up and running. Don't overthink it. Don't get overwhelmed. Just work through this list, one item at a time, and by the end of the week, you'll have a complete AI toolkit ready to go.

The 7-Step Setup Checklist

1. Create a ChatGPT account (free version) Go to chat.openai.com. Sign up with your email or Google account. Spend 15 minutes experimenting. Ask it a question about your field. Ask it to explain something you've been curious about. Get comfortable with the interface. Time required: 20 minutes

2. Try DALL-E (via ChatGPT or the standalone site) If you have ChatGPT Plus, try generating an image directly in ChatGPT. If you're on the free version, go to labs.openai.com and sign up for free credits. Generate at least one image. Describe something specific and see what happens. Time required: 15 minutes

3. Sign up for Notion (free tier) Go to notion.so. Create an account. Explore the templates. Try creating a simple to-do list or a note page. If you want, experiment with Notion AI (you get a few free uses). Time required: 20 minutes

4. Download the Grammarly browser extension Go to grammarly.com. Sign up for a free account. Install the browser extension. Open Gmail or Google Docs and start typing. Watch Grammarly suggest corrections in real-time. Time required: 10 minutes

5. Create a Canva account (free version) Go to canva.com. Sign up. Browse the templates. Try creating a simple social media post or presentation slide. Experiment with the AI features like Magic Write or Background Remover. Time required: 20 minutes

6. Bookmark all of these tools in a dedicated folder Create a folder in your browser called "AI Tools" or "My AI Toolkit." Bookmark ChatGPT, Notion, Canva, Grammarly, and any other tools

you've signed up for. This makes them easy to access whenever you need them.

Time required: 5 minutes

7. Spend 15 minutes experimenting with each tool Don't just sign up and forget about them. Actually, use them. Ask ChatGPT a question. Generate an image with DALL-E. Create a note in Notion. Design something in Canva. Write a paragraph and let Grammarly polish it. The goal isn't to master these tools in one sitting. The goal is to get comfortable with them. To see what they can do. To start building the habit of reaching for AI when you need help. Time required: 1-2 hours total (spread across the week)

Total Time Investment: About 2-3 Hours

That's it. In less time than it takes to binge-watch a few episodes of a TV show, you can have a complete AI toolkit set up and ready to use. And here's the beautiful part: once it's set up, it's there. You don't need to do this again. You just start using the tools whenever you need them.

You're Not Overwhelmed—You're Equipped

I know it might feel like a lot right now. Seven tools. Multiple sign-ups. New interfaces to learn. But here's what I want you to remember: you're not trying to master everything at once. You're just setting up your toolkit. You're just getting the tools in place so they're ready when you need them. Think of it like stocking your kitchen. You don't need to be a master chef to have a knife, a cutting board, and a pan. You just need to have them available so that when you're ready to cook, you're not scrambling to find what you need. Same thing here. You're not trying to become an AI expert overnight. You're just making sure the tools are there when you need them. And trust me—you're going to need them.

You're About to Open Doors You Didn't Even Know Existed

Here's what's going to happen over the next few weeks: You're going to use ChatGPT to solve a problem that would have taken you hours. You're going to generate an image with DALL-E that makes your presentation look 10x more professional. You're going to organize your notes in Notion and finally feel like you're in control of your work. You're going to design something in Canva that actually looks good. You're going to write an email with Grammarly and feel confident hitting send. And each time that happens, you're going to think: Why didn't I start using this sooner? That's the moment I want you to have. That's the realization that changes everything. You're not just learning about AI. You're not just reading about tools. You're actively building the skills and systems that are going to set you apart from everyone else who's still doing things the old way. You're early. You're ahead. And you're equipped. Now let's keep going. End of Chapter 3 In the next chapter, we're going to dive deep into the skill that separates good AI users from great ones: prompt engineering. You've got the tools. Now let's learn how to use them like a pro.

CHAPTER

04

Mastering Prompt Engineering Skill Development

CHAPTER

The Secret That Separates Good Results from Great Results

Let me show you something that's going to blow your mind. Two people. Same AI tool. Same task. Completely different results. Here's the scenario: Both people need ChatGPT to write a marketing email for a product launch. They're both using the free version. They both have the same amount of experience (basically none). They both hit "send" at roughly the same time. Person A types: "Write a marketing email." Person B types: "Write a 150-word marketing email announcing our new productivity app to existing customers. Use a friendly but professional tone. Highlight three key benefits: saves time, reduces stress, integrates with tools they already use. Include a clear call-to-action to download the free trial. Make it feel personal, not corporate. Avoid buzzwords like 'revolutionary' or 'game-changing.'" Now, guess which person gets a generic, forgettable email that sounds like it was written by a robot? And guess which person gets a polished, compelling email they can actually send to customers with minimal editing? If you guessed Person B, you're right. But here's what's wild: they used the exact same tool. Same AI. Same technology. Same capabilities. The only difference? How they asked. This is the secret that separates people getting extraordinary results from AI and people getting... meh results. It's not about having access to better tools. It's not about paying for premium versions (though that helps). It's not about being smarter or more tech-savvy. It's about knowing how to ask. Let me give you an analogy that makes this crystal clear. Imagine you walk into a restaurant. The waiter comes over and asks what you'd like to order.

Option 1: You say, "I want food." The waiter stares at you. "Okay... what kind of food?" "Just... food. Something good." The waiter is confused. Do you want a salad? A steak? Pasta? Are you vegetarian? Do you have allergies? What's your budget? The waiter has no idea what to bring you, so they're either going to keep asking questions or just bring you something random and hope you like it.

Option 2: You say, "I'd like the grilled salmon with steamed vegetables, no butter, lemon on the side. And a side salad with balsamic dressing." The waiter writes it down, heads to the kitchen, and 20 minutes later, you get exactly what you wanted. See the difference? In the first scenario, you're making the waiter do all the work of figuring out what you want. In the second scenario, you're being clear, specific, and helpful. You're making it easy for the waiter to give you exactly what you need. AI works the same way. When you type a vague prompt like "Write a marketing email," you're basically saying "I want food." The AI has to guess what you mean. What kind of email? For what audience? What tone? What length? What's the goal? When you type a specific prompt with context, format, tone, and constraints, you're ordering the grilled salmon with steamed vegetables. You're making it easy for the AI to give you exactly what you need. Here's the thing that most people don't realize: AI is incredibly powerful, but it's not a mind reader. It doesn't know what you're thinking. It doesn't know your goals, your audience, your preferences, or your constraints. It only knows what you tell it. And the better you get at telling it what you want, the better your results become. This is the skill that changes everything. This is the skill that turns AI from "kind of helpful sometimes" to "holy crap, this is saving me hours every week." This skill is called prompt engineering. And I know what you're thinking: That sounds complicated. That sounds technical. That sounds like something I need a computer science degree to understand. Wrong. Prompt engineering is just a fancy term for "knowing how to ask good questions." That's it. If you can order food at a restaurant, you can learn prompt engineering. But here's why it matters so much: this single skill is the multiplier for everything else. You can have access to the best AI tools in the world, but if you don't know how to prompt them effectively, you're only getting 20% of their potential. You're driving a Ferrari in first gear. On the other hand, if you master prompting, even basic AI tools become incredibly powerful. You're squeezing every ounce of value out of the technology. You're getting results that make people ask, "Wait, how did you do that?" Let me give you a real example. Meet Daniel, a 21-year-old college student studying business. He's working on a group project—a marketing plan for a fictional company. His group is struggling to come up with creative campaign ideas. They've been brainstorming for two hours and have nothing good. Daniel decides to try ChatGPT. His first attempt: "Give me marketing ideas." ChatGPT spits out a generic list: "Use social media. Run ads. Offer discounts. Partner with influencers." Daniel is disappointed. This is useless. I could have Googled this. But then he remembers something he read about being more specific.

He tries again: "I'm working on a marketing campaign for a fictional eco-friendly water bottle company targeting college students aged 18-24. Our unique selling point is that the bottles are made from 100% recycled ocean plastic. Give me 10 creative, low-budget marketing campaign ideas that would resonate with environmentally-conscious Gen Z students. For each idea, explain why it would work and how to execute it." This time, ChatGPT delivers. It suggests a campus cleanup challenge where students collect plastic waste and get discounts. It proposes a social media campaign showing the journey of ocean plastic becoming a water bottle. It recommends partnering with environmental clubs and hosting "Refill Stations" at campus events. Every idea is specific, actionable, and actually creative. Daniel brings these ideas to his group. They're blown away. They pick three of the ideas, refine them, and end up with the best project in the class. Same tool. Same student. Completely different results. The only thing that changed? How Daniel asked the question. That's the power of prompt engineering. And here's the best part: this is a learnable skill. You don't need to be naturally good at it. You don't need special training. You just need to understand the principles and practice applying them. By the end of this chapter, you're going to know exactly how to craft prompts that get you extraordinary results. You're going to understand the anatomy of a perfect prompt.

You're going to learn advanced techniques that most people don't even know exist. And you're going to have a 12-week roadmap to go from beginner to expert. This is the skill that separates good AI users from great ones. Let's learn how to ask like a pro.

The Anatomy of a Perfect Prompt

Alright, let's break this down. If you want to consistently get great results from AI, you need to understand what makes a prompt effective. And the good news is, there's a formula. It's not complicated. It's not mysterious. It's just a framework—a checklist of elements that, when combined, produce high-quality outputs. Think of it like a recipe. If you're baking a cake, you need flour, eggs, sugar, butter, and baking powder. Miss one ingredient, and your cake doesn't turn out right. But if you include all the ingredients in the right proportions, you get a delicious cake every time. Prompts work the same way. Here are the six key ingredients of a perfect prompt:

1. Context/Role: Set the Stage

The first thing you need to do is give the AI context. What's the situation? What's your background? What's the AI's role in this interaction? Think of this as setting the stage for a conversation. If you walk up to someone and immediately start talking about a problem without any context, they're going to be confused. But if you say, "Hey, I'm working on a school project about climate change, and I need help brainstorming ideas," now they understand the situation and can help you more effectively. AI needs the same thing. Bad example (no context): "Write an email." Good example (with context): "I'm a freelance graphic designer reaching out to a potential client who expressed interest in my work last month. Write a follow-up email." See the difference? In the second version, the AI knows who you are, who you're writing to, and what the relationship is. That context shapes the entire response. You can also assign the AI a role.

This is incredibly powerful. Example: "You are an experienced career coach. I'm a recent college graduate trying to decide between two job offers. Help me think through the pros and cons." By telling the AI to act as a career coach, you're priming it to respond with that perspective. It's going to give you thoughtful, strategic advice rather than generic information. Key takeaway: Always start your prompt with context. Who are you? What's the situation? What role should the AI play?

2. The Ask: Be Specific About What You Want

This is the core of your prompt. What exactly do you want the AI to do? The more specific you are, the better your results. Vague ask: "Help me with my resume." What does "help" mean? Rewrite it? Give feedback? Suggest improvements? The AI has no idea. Specific ask: "Review my resume and suggest three specific improvements to make it more appealing to tech startups. Focus on the skills and experience sections." Now the AI knows exactly what to do. It's going to review your resume, focus on specific sections, and provide actionable suggestions tailored to tech startups. Here's another example: Vague ask: "Explain quantum physics." Specific ask: "Explain the concept of quantum entanglement in simple terms, as if I'm a high school student with no physics background. Use an analogy to make it easier to understand." The second version tells the AI exactly what concept to explain, what level of complexity to use, and even suggests using an analogy. The result is going to be way more useful. Key takeaway: Don't make the AI guess what you want. Be explicit. The more specific your ask, the better your output.

3. Format: How Should the Response Be Structured?

Do you want a paragraph? A bullet-point list? A table? A step-by-step guide? An essay? Specifying the format helps the AI organize information in the way that's most useful to you. Example without format: "Give me tips for studying effectively." You'll probably get a paragraph or two of general advice. Example with format: "Give me 10 tips for studying effectively, formatted as a numbered list. For each tip, include one sentence explaining why it works." Now you're going to get a clean, organized list that's easy to scan and reference. Here's another example: Without format: "Compare the benefits of remote work vs. office work." With format: "Create a table comparing remote work and office work. Include columns for: Productivity, Work-Life Balance, Collaboration, and Cost. Use 2-3 bullet points per cell." The second version gives you a structured, visual comparison that's immediately useful. Key takeaway: Tell the AI how you want the information presented. Format matters.

4. Tone: What Voice Should the AI Use?

Tone is huge. The same information can sound completely different depending on how it's delivered. Do you want the AI to sound professional? Casual? Friendly? Formal? Humorous? Motivational? Example: "Write a LinkedIn post about the importance of networking." Without specifying tone, you might get something generic and corporate. Better example: "Write a LinkedIn post about the importance of networking. Use a conversational, authentic tone—like you're giving advice to a friend, not delivering a corporate presentation. Keep it under 150 words." Now the AI knows to avoid stiff, formal language and write something that feels genuine and relatable. Here's another example: Without tone: "Write a rejection email to a job candidate." With tone: "Write a rejection email to a job candidate. Use a kind, respectful tone that acknowledges their effort and encourages them to apply again in the future. Avoid corporate jargon." The second version ensures the email doesn't sound cold or dismissive. Key takeaway: Tone shapes how your message is received. Always specify the voice you want.

5. Constraints: Set the Boundaries

Constraints are the guardrails that keep the AI focused. They tell the AI what NOT to do, or what limits to work within. Common constraints include:

- Word count or length
- Complexity level (simple vs. advanced)
- Topics to avoid
- Specific requirements (must include X, must

avoid Y) Example without constraints: "Write a blog post about productivity." You might get a 2,000-word essay that's way too long and covers topics you don't care about. Example with constraints: "Write a 500-word blog post about productivity tips for remote workers. Keep the language simple and actionable. Avoid clichés like 'work smarter, not harder.' Focus on practical, specific advice." Now the AI knows exactly what to include, what to avoid, and how long the post should be. Here's another example: Without constraints:

"Explain how to start a business." With constraints: "Explain how to start a business in 5 steps. Assume the reader has no prior business experience and a budget under $1,000. Keep each step under 100 words." The constraints make the response focused, practical, and accessible. Key takeaway: Constraints prevent the AI from going off-track. They keep the response tight and relevant.

6. Examples: Show, Don't Just Tell (Optional but Powerful)

This is the secret weapon of advanced prompt engineering.

If you want the AI to match a specific style, voice, or format, the best way to communicate that is by showing examples. Example: "Write three social media captions for my coffee shop. Here are examples of the style I like:

1. 'Rainy mornings hit different with a warm latte in hand

2. 'That 3pm slump? We've got you covered. Swing by for a pick-me-up.'

3. 'New seasonal menu alert: Pumpkin spice is BACK and better than ever Now write 5 more captions in the same style for our new cold brew launch." By providing examples, you're teaching the AI exactly what you want. It can match the tone, the structure, the emoji usage, the length—everything. This technique is called "few-shot prompting," and it's incredibly effective for maintaining consistency. Key takeaway: When you want a specific style or format, show the AI examples. It's the fastest way to get exactly what you want.

Putting It All Together: Before and After

Let's see what happens when you apply all six elements. Before (vague prompt): "Write a cover letter." After (perfect prompt): "I'm a recent college graduate with a degree in marketing, applying for a social media coordinator position at a tech startup. Write a cover letter that highlights my internship experience managing Instagram and TikTok accounts, my passion for digital storytelling, and my eagerness to learn. Use a professional but enthusiastic tone. Keep it under 300 words. Avoid clichés like 'I'm a hard worker' or 'I'm a team player.' Instead, focus on specific examples and results." The second version includes:

- Context: Recent grad, marketing degree, applying for social media role
- The Ask: Write a cover letter highlighting specific experiences
- Format: Cover letter, under 300 words
- Tone: Professional but enthusiastic Constraints: Avoid clichés, focus on examples and results. The result? A cover letter that's tailored, specific, and actually usable. Here's another example: Before: "Explain blockchain." After: "Explain blockchain technology in simple terms, as if I'm a 12-year-old with no technical background. Use an analogy involving something familiar, like a notebook or a game. Keep the explanation under 200 words. Focus on what it is and why it matters, not the technical details." The second version includes:
- Context: Explaining to a 12-year-old with no tech background
- The Ask: Explain what blockchain is and why it matters
- Format: Simple explanation under 200 words

- Tone: Simple, accessible language
- Constraints: Use an analogy, avoid technical jargon Examples: Suggested analogy direction (notebook or game) The result? An explanation that's clear, memorable, and actually understandable.

The More Specific You Are, the Better Your Results

Here's the pattern you need to internalize: specificity = quality. Every time you add detail to your prompt, you're increasing the likelihood of getting a great result. Vague prompts produce vague results. Specific prompts produce specific, useful, high-quality results. And here's the beautiful part: this isn't hard. You're not learning a programming language. You're not memorizing complex syntax. You're just learning to communicate clearly. Think about it this way: if you were delegating a task to a human assistant, you'd give them clear instructions, right? You'd tell them what you need, why you need it, how you want it formatted, and what to avoid. AI is the same. It's just an assistant that happens to be software instead of a person. The better you get at giving instructions, the better your assistant performs. So, here's your challenge: the next time you use ChatGPT (or any AI tool), don't just type the first thing that comes to mind. Pause. Think about the six elements. Add context. Be specific about what you want. Specify the format and tone. Set constraints. It might take you an extra 30 seconds to write a better prompt. But that 30 seconds will save you 10 minutes of editing and revising the output. That's the trade-off. And it's 100% worth it.

Advanced Prompting Techniques: Roleplay, Chain-of-Thought, Few-Shot Examples

Alright, you've got the basics down. You understand the anatomy of a good prompt. You know how to add context, be specific, set the format, define the tone, and include constraints. Now let's level up. There are three advanced techniques that will take your prompting from good to exceptional. These are the techniques that separate casual AI users from people who are getting truly extraordinary results. And here's the thing: they sound complicated, but they're actually simple. You're going to read about them, try them once, and think, Wait, that's it? That's the "advanced" technique? Yes. That's it. The magic isn't in the complexity. The magic is in knowing these techniques exist and remembering to use them. Let's dive in.

Technique 1: Roleplay / Assume a Persona

This is one of the most powerful techniques in prompt engineering, and it's shockingly simple. Here's the idea: instead of just asking the AI a question, you tell it to respond as if it's a specific person, profession, or character. Why does this work? Because it primes the AI to think from a particular perspective. It activates a specific "mode" of thinking. Example: Basic prompt: "Give me feedback on my business idea." You'll get generic feedback. "That sounds interesting. You should do market research. Consider your target audience." Roleplay prompt: "You are a skeptical venture capitalist who has seen thousands of startup pitches. I'm pitching you my business idea: a subscription service for personalized meal kits targeting busy professionals. Give me brutally honest feedback. What are the biggest weaknesses in this idea? What would make you say no?" Now you're going to get sharp, critical feedback that actually helps you improve your idea. The AI is thinking like an investor, not just a generic advisor. Here's another example: Basic prompt: "Help me write a cold email to a potential client." Roleplay prompt: "You are a successful freelance copywriter who has landed dozens of high-paying clients through cold emails. Write a cold email for me, a beginner freelances graphic designer, reaching out to a small business owner who might need branding work. Make it personal, not salesy, and include a clear call-to-action." The second version is going to give you a much better email because the AI is thinking from the perspective of someone who's actually done this successfully. Real-world example: Meet Sofia, a 24-year-old freelance writer. She's been using ChatGPT to help her write pitches to potential clients, but the pitches always feel generic. They're not bad, but they're not great either. Then she learns about roleplay prompting. She tries this: "You are a busy marketing director at a mid-size tech company. You receive 20+ cold pitches from freelancers every week. I'm a freelance writer pitching my services. Write a pitch email that would actually catch your attention and make you want to reply. Explain why this approach works." The result? A pitch that's concise, value-focused, and actually interesting. Sofia starts using this approach for all her pitches. Her response rate triples. When to use roleplay prompting:

- When you need a specific perspective (investor, customer, expert, critic)
- When you want specialized advice
- When you're writing for a specific audience and want to understand their mindset
- When you want to challenge your own

assumptions Key takeaway: Telling the AI to assume a persona unlocks a different level of thinking. Use it whenever you want specialized, perspective-driven responses.

Technique 2: Chain-of-Thought (Break Down Complex Thinking)

This technique is all about asking the AI to show its work. Instead of just giving you an answer, you ask it to explain its reasoning step-by-step. You ask it to walk you through how it arrived at the conclusion. Why does this work? Two reasons: 1. It forces the AI to think more carefully and logically 2. It helps you understand the reasoning, which makes the answer more useful Example: Basic prompt: "Should I take this job offer?" You'll get a generic response: "It depends on your priorities. Consider the salary, growth opportunities, and work-life balance." Chain-of-thought prompt: "I have two job offers. Job A pays $60k, has great benefits, but limited growth potential. Job B pays $ 5 0k, fewer benefits, but lots of learning opportunities and a clear path to promotion. I'm 23, single, and my main goal is career growth over the next 5 years. Walk me through how to think about this decision step-by-step. What factors should I weigh? What questions should I ask myself?" Now the AI is going to break down the decision-making process. It's going to help you think through the trade-offs systematically. Here's another example: Basic prompt: "How do I solve this math problem: If a train leaves Station A at 60 mph and another train leaves Station B at 80 mph, and they're 420 miles apart, when will they meet?" Chain-of-thought prompt: "Solve this math problem step-by-step.

Show your work and explain each step so I can understand the logic: If a train leaves Station A at 60 mph and another train leaves Station B at 80 mph, and they're 420 miles apart, when will they meet?" The second version doesn't just give you the answer (3 hours). It shows you how to set up the equation, why you add the speeds, and how to solve for time. You actually learn something. Real-world example: Meet Kevin, a 20-year-old computer science student. He's stuck on a coding problem for his class. He's been staring at his code for an hour and can't figure out why it's not working. He pastes his code into ChatGPT and asks: "Why isn't this code working?" ChatGPT points out the error, but Kevin doesn't really understand why it's an error.

He fixes it, but he hasn't learned anything. Then he tries chain-of-thought prompting: "Here's my code: [code]. It's supposed to sort a list of numbers, but it's giving me an error. Walk me through what's happening step-by-step. Explain what each part of the code is doing, where the error is occurring, why it's happening, and how to fix it." This time, ChatGPT breaks down the code line by line. It explains the logic, identifies the error, explains why it's causing a problem, and shows how to fix it. Kevin doesn't just fix the bug—he understands what went wrong and how to avoid it in the future. When to use chain-of-thought prompting:

- When you're learning something new and want to understand the logic When you're solving complex problems
- When you want to verify the AI's reasoning
- When you need to explain something to someone else Key takeaway: Adding "explain your reasoning step-by-step" or

"walk me through your thinking" dramatically improves the quality and usefulness of AI responses.

Technique 3: Few-Shot Examples (Teach by Example)

This is the technique that gives you the most control over the AI's output. Here's how it works: instead of just describing what you want, you show the AI examples of what you want. You teach it by demonstration. The AI is incredibly good at recognizing patterns. If you show it 2-3 examples of the style, format, or tone you want, it can replicate that pattern for new content. Example: Basic prompt: "Write social media captions for my fitness coaching business." You'll get generic captions that could apply to any fitness business. Few-shot prompt: "I run a fitness coaching business. Here are three examples of captions I've written that performed well:

1. 'You don't need a perfect plan. You just need to start. One workout today is better than a perfect plan you never execute.

2. 'Sore muscles are just your body's way of saying: we're getting stronger. Embrace the discomfort—it's temporary, but the results last.

3. 'Consistency & Intensity. Showing up 3x a week for a year beat going hard for a month and burning out. Play the long game.' Now write 5 more captions in the same style and tone for my upcoming posts about nutrition, recovery, and mindset." The AI is going to match your voice, your structure, your use of emojis, your message style—everything. The captions will sound like you wrote them. Here's another example: Basic prompt: "Write product

descriptions for my online store." Few-shot prompt: "I sell handmade candles.

Here are two product descriptions I've written:

1. 'Lavender Dreams: Hand-poured soy candle with pure lavender essential oil. Burns for 40+ hours. Perfect for winding down after a long day. Light it, breathe deep, and let the stress melt away.'

2. 'Citrus Sunrise: Bright, energizing blend of orange and grapefruit. Fills your space with morning energy (even if it's 3pm). Burns clean for 40+ hours. Your new favorite pick-me-up.' Now write descriptions for these three new scents: Vanilla Chai, Ocean Breeze, and Forest Pine. Match the style, tone, and length of the examples above." The AI is going to produce descriptions that fit seamlessly with your existing product line.

Real-world example: Meet Jasmine, a 26-year-old content creator who runs a personal finance blog. She's been using ChatGPT to help her write blog posts, but the AI's writing style doesn't quite match her voice. It's too formal, too generic. Then she discovers few-shot prompting. She takes three of her best-performing blog posts, pulls out the opening paragraphs, and uses them as examples Now write the opening paragraph for a new blog post about 'How to Save Money on Groceries Without Eating Ramen Every Night.' Match the tone, style, and structure of the examples above." The result? An opening paragraph that sounds exactly like Jasmine wrote it. She barely has to edit it. She starts using this technique for all her content. Her writing process speeds up, and her blog maintains a consistent voice across every post. When to use few-shot prompting: When you want to maintain a consistent brand voice

- When you're creating content in a specific style

or format When you want the AI to match your personal

writing style

- When you're producing content at scale and

need consistency Key takeaway: Examples are the fastest way to teach the AI exactly what you want. Show, don't just tell.

Combining Techniques: The Power of Stacking

Here's where it gets really powerful: you can combine these techniques. You can use roleplay + chain-of-thought. You can use few-shot examples + constraints. You can use all three at once. Example of stacking: "You are an experienced email marketer who has written hundreds of high-converting sales emails. I need to write an email promoting a 20% discount on my online course about productivity. Here are two examples of emails I've written that got good results Now write a new email in the same style. Walk me through your thinking: explain why you're making specific word choices, why you're structuring it this way, and what psychological principles you're using to drive conversions. Keep it under 200 words." This prompt combines:

- Roleplay: "You are an experienced email marketer"
- Few-shot examples: Providing two example emails
- Chain-of-thought: "Walk me through your thinking"
- Constraints: "Keep it under 200 words"

The result? An email that's perfectly tailored to your style, with a detailed explanation of why it works. Real-world example: Meet Alex, a 28-year-old freelance developer. He's building a portfolio website and needs to write compelling copy for his services page. He's not a writer, and every draft he creates feels awkward. He decides to use all three advanced techniques: "You are a professional copywriter specializing in freelancer websites. Here are two examples of service descriptions from successful freelance developers: Now write a service description for my web development services. I specialize in building custom websites for small businesses using React and Node.js. My unique value is that I focus on speed and user experience, not just aesthetics. Write in a confident but approachable tone. Explain your reasoning step-by-step: why you're emphasizing certain benefits, what psychological triggers you're using, and how you're differentiating me from other developers. Keep it under 150 words." The result? A service description that's professional, persuasive, and sounds like it was written by a pro. Plus, Alex learns why it works, so he can apply those principles to other parts of his website. Key takeaway: These techniques aren't mutually exclusive. Stack them for even better results.

These Techniques Turn Basic AI Interaction Into True Collaboration

Here's what I want you to understand: when you use these advanced techniques, you're not just using AI as a tool. You're collaborating with it. You're teaching it your style. You're guiding its thinking. You're shaping the output to match your exact needs. It stops feeling like you're talking to a robot and starts feeling like you're working with a really smart assistant who understands what you want. And that's when AI becomes truly powerful. So, here's your challenge: pick one of these techniques and try it today. Ask

ChatGPT to assume a persona. Ask it to explain its reasoning step-by-step. Show it examples of what you want and ask it to create more. You're going to be shocked at how much better your results become.

Practice Scenarios: Real-World Prompting Across Four Domains

Alright, enough theory. Let's get practical. I'm going to walk you through four real-world scenarios—situations you're likely to encounter in school, work, or your personal projects. For each scenario, I'll show you three versions of the prompt: basic, better, and advanced. You'll see exactly how the quality of your prompt affects the quality of the output. And you'll get sample prompts you can copy, modify, and use immediately. Think of this section as your prompt library. Bookmark it. Come back to it. Use these as templates for your own work. Let's go.

Scenario 1: Copywriting & Content Creation

Situation: You're launching a side business selling custom phone cases online. You need product descriptions that are compelling, concise, and convert browsers into buyers. Basic Prompt: "Write product descriptions for my phone cases." What you'll get: Generic descriptions that could apply to any phone case. "This phone case is durable and stylish. It protects your phone from drops and scratches. Available in multiple colors." Boring. Forgettable. Not compelling. Better Prompt: "I sell custom-designed phone cases featuring original artwork. My target audience is 18-30-year-olds who care about self-expression and aesthetics. Write a product description for a phone case with a floral watercolour design. Use a friendly, enthusiastic tone. Highlight the unique design, the protective features, and the fact that it's a conversation starter. Keep it under 100 words." What you'll get: A much better description that's specific, targeted, and actually interesting. It speaks to the audience's values (self-expression, aesthetics) and emphasizes benefits (protection + style). Advanced Prompt: "You are a professional e-commerce copywriter who specializes in lifestyle products. I sell custom-designed phone cases. Here are two product descriptions I've written that converted well:

1. 'Midnight Garden: Hand-illustrated florals meet serious protection. This case isn't just pretty—it's tough. Shock-absorbent edges, raised bezels to protect your screen, and a design that makes people ask, "Where'd you get that?" Available for iPhone and Samsung.

2. 'Desert Sunset: Warm tones, bold lines, and a vibe that says you don't follow trends—you set them. Military-grade drop protection wrapped in art. Your phone deserves better than basic black.' Now write a product description for a new design: 'Ocean Waves' (abstract blue and teal waves). Match the tone, style, and structure of the examples above. Explain your reasoning: why you're emphasizing certain features, what emotional triggers you're using, and how you're differentiating this from generic phone cases." What you'll get: A description that perfectly matches your brand voice, emphasizes the right features, and includes an explanation of the copywriting strategy. You can use it immediately, and you've learned something about what makes good copy work. Common mistakes to avoid:

- Being too vague about your audience
- Not specifying tone (formal? casual? playful?)

- Forgetting to mention what makes your product unique
- Not setting a word count (you'll get descriptions

that are way too long) Takeaway: The advanced version gives you professional-quality copy you can use immediately, plus insights into why it works.

Scenario 2: Coding & Technical Problems

Situation: You're working on a Python project for school. Your code is supposed to read a CSV file and calculate the average of a column, but you're getting an error and you don't know why. Basic Prompt: "Debug this code: [paste code]" What you'll get: The AI might identify the error and suggest a fix, but you won't understand why it was wrong or how to avoid it in the future. Better Prompt: "I'm working on a Python script that reads a CSV file and calculates the average of the 'sales' column. Here's my code: [paste code]. I'm getting this error: [paste error message]. I've tried [what you've already tried]. Can you identify the problem and explain what's causing it?" What you'll get: A more targeted response. The AI understands the context (what the code is supposed to do), sees the error message, and knows what you've already tried. The explanation will be more helpful. Advanced Prompt: "I'm a beginner Python programmer working on a data analysis project. My code is supposed to read a CSV file and calculate the average of the 'sales' column. Here's my code: [paste code]. I'm getting this error: [paste error message]. Walk me through what's happening step-by-step: explain what each part of my code is doing, where the error is occurring, why it's happening, and how to fix it. Also, suggest best practices to avoid this type of error in the future. Explain your reasoning in simple terms—I'm still learning." What you'll get: A detailed, educational response. The AI will break down your code line by line, explain the error in simple terms, show you how to fix it, and teach you how to avoid similar problems. You're not just fixing the bug—you're learning. Common mistakes to avoid:

- Not including the error message (the AI needs to see the actual error)
- Not explaining what the code is supposed to do (context matters) Not mentioning what you've already tried (saves time)
- Asking for a fix without asking for an explanation (you won't learn anything) Takeaway: With the advanced approach, you don't just get a fix—you understand what went wrong and how to prevent it next time.

Scenario 3: Research & Summarization

Situation: You're writing a research paper on the impact of social media on mental health. You need to understand the current research landscape and synthesize key findings. Basic Prompt: "What is the impact of social media on mental health?" What you'll get: A generic overview. "Studies show that social media can have both positive and negative effects on mental health. Some research suggests it increases anxiety and depression, while other studies show it can provide social support." Not specific enough. Not actionable. Better Prompt: "I'm writing a research paper on the impact of social media on mental health among teenagers (ages 13-18). Summarize the key findings from recent research (last 5 years). Focus on:

1) negative effects (anxiety, depression, sleep issues),

2) positive effects (social connection, support networks), and

3) factors that determine whether the impact is positive or negative (usage patterns, content type, etc.).

Organize the information in a clear, structured format." What you'll get: A much more useful summary. The AI knows your specific focus (teenagers), the time frame (last 5 years), and the structure you want (negative effects, positive effects, determining factors). The response will be organized and actionable. Advanced Prompt: "You are a research psychologist specializing in adolescent mental health and technology use. I'm writing a research paper on the impact of social media on mental health among teenagers (ages 13-18). Provide a comprehensive summary of recent research (last 5 years) organized into three sections:

1. Negative effects: What are the most well-documented harms? What mechanisms explain these effects?

2. Positive effects: What benefits have been identified? Under what conditions do these benefits occur?

3. Nuance and context: What factors determine whether social media use is harmful or beneficial? (e.g., passive vs. active use, time spent, type of content, individual vulnerabilities) For each section, cite 2-3 key studies or meta-analyses. Explain the findings in accessible language suitable for an undergraduate research paper. Also, identify any gaps in the current research or areas of ongoing debate. Walk me through your reasoning: why are you highlighting these particular studies? What makes them significant?" What you'll get: A comprehensive, well-organized summary that's ready to use in your paper. The AI is thinking like a subject matter expert, highlighting the most important research, explaining the nuances, and even

identifying gaps in the literature. Plus, you get an explanation of why these studies matter. Common mistakes to avoid:

- Being too broad (specify your exact focus)
- Not specifying the time frame (recent research vs. historical)
- Not requesting a specific structure (you'll get a wall of text)
- Not asking for sources or citations (you need to verify the information) Takeaway: You're turning general information into specifically useful intelligence that's ready to use in your work.

Scenario 4: Brainstorming Ideation

Situation: You're a content creator trying to come up with fresh video ideas for your YouTube channel about personal finance. You're stuck and need inspiration. Basic Prompt: "Give me content ideas for my YouTube channel." What you'll get: Generic ideas that have been done a thousand times. "How to save money. Budgeting tips. Investing for beginners." Not helpful. Not original. Better Prompt: "I run a YouTube channel about personal finance for people in their 20s. My audience is young professionals and recent graduates who are just starting to think about money. I want to create content that's practical, relatable, and not preachy. Give me 10 video ideas that are specific, actionable, and haven't been done to death. For each idea, include a brief description of what the video would cover." What you'll get: Much better ideas that are tailored to your audience and niche. The AI understands who you're creating for and what tone you want. The ideas will be more specific and actionable. Advanced Prompt: "You are a successful YouTube content strategist who specializes in personal finance channels. I run a channel targeting people in their

20s—young professionals and recent graduates who are just starting to manage money. My most successful videos have been: 'I Tracked Every Dollar I Spent for 30 Days' (practical experiment), 'Why I Don't Follow the 50/30/20 Rule' (challenging conventional advice), and 'How I Automated My Savings Without Thinking About It' (actionable systems). Give me 10 new video ideas that would resonate with my audience. For each idea:

1. Provide a compelling title

2. Explain the core concept (what makes it interesting/unique)

3. Suggest a hook for the first 30 seconds

4. Explain why this idea would perform well (what psychological triggers or audience needs does it address) Focus on ideas that are fresh, not overdone, and that play to my strengths: personal experiments, challenging conventional wisdom, and practical systems. Avoid generic advice like 'budgeting 101' or 'investing basics.'" What you'll get: Ten highly specific, original video ideas with titles, hooks, and strategic reasoning. Each idea is tailored to your audience and your content style. You can immediately start scripting and filming. Plus, you understand why each idea would work, which helps you develop your content strategy. Common mistakes to avoid:

- Not specifying your niche or audience (you'll get

generic ideas) Not mentioning what's worked for you in the past

(the AI can't build on your strengths)

- Not setting constraints (you'll get ideas that have

been done a million times) Not asking for reasoning (you won't understand

why the ideas would work) Takeaway: Advanced prompting turns generic ideas into actionable, original concepts that are ready to execute.

The Pattern You Should Notice

Look at what happened in each scenario: Basic prompts gave you generic, forgettable results. Better prompts gave you useful, targeted results by adding context, specificity, and structure. Advanced prompts gave you professional-quality results by combining roleplay, examples, chain-of-thought reasoning, and strategic constraints. The difference isn't the AI tool. The difference is how you asked. And here's the beautiful part: once you've written a great prompt for a specific task, you can save it and reuse it. You're building a library of prompts that work. So here's your action step: pick one of these scenarios (or a similar situation you're facing), and try writing an advanced prompt. Use the templates above as a starting point. Modify them to fit your specific needs. You're going to be amazed at the results.

Your 12-Week AI Skill Development Roadmap

Alright, you've learned the fundamentals. You understand the anatomy of a perfect prompt. You know the advanced techniques. You've seen real-world examples. Now comes the most important part: practice. Here's the truth: reading about prompt engineering is useful, but it won't make you good at it. The only way to get good is to actually do it. Consistently. Over time. Think of it like learning a language. You can read all the grammar books you want, but you won't become fluent until you start speaking. You need repetition. You need practice. You need to make mistakes and learn from them. Prompt engineering is the same. The good news? You don't need to practice for years. You don't even need to practice for months. With focused, consistent practice, you can go from beginner to advanced in about 12 weeks. That's three months. 90 days. Less time than a college semester. And here's the key: 15-30 minutes per day of consistent practice beats occasional intense effort every single time. You're not trying to become an expert overnight. You're trying to build a skill gradually, one day at a time. So here's your roadmap. This is a week-by-week plan that will take you from "I'm not sure how to ask AI for what I want" to "I consistently get professional-quality results on the first try." Let's break it down.

Weeks 1-2: Foundation Basics

Goal: Learn the anatomy of good prompts and get comfortable being specific. What you're learning:

- The six elements of a perfect prompt (context, ask, format, tone, constraints, examples)
- How to add context to your prompts
- How to be specific about what you want
- How to specify format and tone

Daily practice (15-20 minutes):

- Write 3-5 prompts per day for different tasks (writing, research, brainstorming, problem-solving)
- Before you hit enter, review your prompt: Did

you include context? Are you being specific? Did you specify format and tone?

- Compare your results to what you would have gotten with a vague prompt Weekly goal:
- By the end of week 2, you should feel comfortable adding context and being specific in your prompts
- You should notice that your AI results are significantly better than when you started Success metric:
- 50% of your prompts produce results that are immediately useful (even if they need minor tweaking) Example practice tasks:
- Day 1: Write a prompt to help you draft an email
- Day 2: Write a prompt to explain a concept you're learning
- Day 3: Write a prompt to brainstorm ideas for a project
- Day 4: Write a prompt to get feedback on something you've written
- Day 5: Write a prompt to help you solve a problem you're facing Reflection question (end of week 2): "What's the biggest difference I've noticed in my AI results since I started being more specific in my prompts?"

Weeks 3-4: Adding Complexity

Goal: Learn and practice advanced techniques (roleplay, chain of-thought). What you're learning:

- How to use roleplay/persona prompting
- How to ask for step-by-step reasoning
- When to use each technique

- How to combine techniques

Daily practice (20-25 minutes):

- Try roleplay prompting at least 3 times this week

(ask the AI to respond as a specific person or profession)

- Try chain-of-thought prompting at least 3 times

this week (ask the AI to explain its reasoning step-by-step)

- Experiment with combining these techniques

with the basics you learned in weeks 1-2 Weekly goal:

- By the end of week 4, you should understand

when to use roleplay and when to use chain-of-thought

- You should be getting expert-level perspectives

and detailed explanations from AI Success metric:

- You can consistently get AI to respond from a

specific perspective

- You can get AI to explain complex concepts in a

way you actually understand Example practice tasks:

- Day 1: Ask AI to respond as a career coach and

give you advice

- Day 2: Ask AI to explain a difficult concept

step-by-step

- Day 3: Ask AI to respond as a skeptical

customer and critique your pitch Day 4: Ask AI to walk you through solving a

problem step-by-step

- Day 5: Combine roleplay + chain-of-thought in a

single prompt Reflection question (end of week 4): "Which advanced technique (roleplay or chain-of-thought) has been most useful for me? Why?"

Weeks 5-6: Experimentation & Refinement

Goal: Combine all techniques and start building a personal prompt library. What you're learning:

- How to stack techniques for maximum impact
- How to refine prompts that didn't work the first time
- How to identify patterns in what works for you
- How to save and organize successful prompts

Daily practice (25-30 minutes): Write prompts that combine multiple techniques (anatomy + roleplay + chain-of-thought)

- When a prompt doesn't produce great results, refine it and try again Start a "prompt journal" or document where you save prompts that worked well
- Organize your prompts by category (writing, research, brainstorming, problem-solving, etc.) Weekly goal: By the end of week 6, 80% of your prompts should produce usable results on the first try
- You should have a growing library of prompts you can reuse Success metric: You're saving meaningful time on real tasks

(emails, research, content creation, etc.)

- You rarely need to ask the AI the same question twice because you got it right the first time Example practice tasks:

- Day 1: Write a complex prompt combining all techniques for a real task you need to complete
- Day 2: Take a prompt that didn't work well and refine it until it does
- Day 3: Create a template prompt for a task you do regularly (e.g., writing emails, brainstorming ideas)
- Day 4: Organize your successful prompts into categories
- Day 5: Test your template prompts on new tasks to see if they're reusable Reflection question (end of week 6): "What types of prompts work best for me? What patterns have I noticed in my successful prompts?"

Weeks 7-8: Few-Shot Examples & Pattern Training

Goal: Master the art of teaching AI your style through examples. What you're learning: How to use few-shot prompting (providing

examples)

- How to maintain consistent voice and style across AI outputs How to create custom templates for recurring tasks
- How to train AI to match your personal style Daily practice (25-30 minutes): Collect examples of good writing, design, or content in your field
- Practice few-shot prompting: show AI 2-3 examples and ask it to create more in the same style
- Create templates for tasks you do regularly (social media posts, emails, blog outlines, etc.) Test whether AI can consistently match your style Weekly goal:
- By the end of week 8, AI outputs should require

minimal editing You should have a consistent brand voice/style across all AI-generated content Success metric:

- People can't tell the difference between content you wrote and content AI helped you write (because it matches your voice perfectly) You have reusable templates for your most common tasks Example practice tasks:
- Day 1: Collect 3 examples of your best writing and use them in a few-shot prompt Day 2: Create a template for social media captions using few-shot examples
- Day 3: Create a template for email responses using few-shot examples Day 4: Test your templates on new content to see if the style is consistent
- Day 5: Refine your templates based on what worked and what didn't Reflection question (end of week 8): "How much editing do my AI outputs require now compared to when I started? What's changed?"

Weeks 9-10: Domain-Specific Mastery

Goal: Deep dive into your specific use case and become an expert in that domain. What you're learning:

- Advanced prompting techniques specific to your field (copywriting, coding, research, design, etc.)
- How successful people in your field are using AI
- Domain-specific best practices and common pitfalls
- How to push the boundaries of what AI can do in your area Daily practice (30 minutes):

- Focus exclusively on prompts related to your field or primary use case
- Study successful prompts from others in your field (search online, join communities, ask peers)
- Experiment with advanced techniques specific to your domain
- Push the limits: try to get AI to do things you weren't sure it could do Weekly goal:
- By the end of week 10, you should be getting expert-level results in your specific domain
- You should be working 2-3x faster than you were before you started using AI Success metric:
- You're consistently producing professional-quality work with AI assistance
- You've found creative uses for AI that others in your field haven't thought of Example practice tasks:
- Day 1: Research how top performers in your field are using AI
- Day 2: Try to replicate their techniques with your own prompts
- Day 3: Experiment with a use case you haven't tried before
- Day 4: Push the boundaries: ask AI to do something you're not sure it can do
- Day 5: Refine your domain-specific prompt templates Reflection question (end of week 10): "What's the most surprising or creative way I've used AI in my field? What results did it produce?"

Weeks 11-12: Advanced Integration &Workflow

Goal: Make AI a natural, seamless part of your workflow. What you're learning: How to integrate AI into your daily routine without it feeling like extra work

- How to build AI-powered workflows for complex tasks How to measure and track your productivity gains
- How to continue improving beyond the 12-week mark Daily practice (30 minutes): Use AI naturally throughout your day (not as a separate "practice" session)
- Build workflows that combine multiple AI tools (e.g., ChatGPT for writing + Canva for design) Track your time savings and productivity gains
- Experiment with new techniques and tools

Final goal:

- By the end of week 12, AI should feel like a natural part of how you work, not an additional step
- You should be able to articulate exactly how AI has improved your productivity and results Success metric:
- You can't imagine working without AI now
- You're consistently saving 5-10+ hours per week
- You're producing higher-quality work in less time

Example practice tasks: Day 1: Build a workflow for a complex task (e.g., creating a blog post from research to publication)

- Day 2: Track your time for a full day and measure how much time AI saved you

- Day 3: Teach someone else how to use AI effectively (teaching reinforces learning)
- Day 4: Experiment with a new AI tool or technique you haven't tried before
- Day 5: Reflect on your 12-week journey and plan your next 90 days Final reflection (end of week 12): "How has my work changed over the past 12 weeks? What can I do now that I couldn't do before? What's next?"

Key Principles Throughout the 12 Weeks

1. Consistency & Intensity 15-30 minutes every day beats 3 hours once a week. Build the habit. Make it part of your routine.

2. Keep a Prompt Journal Record prompts that work. Note why they worked. Build a library you can reference and reuse.

3. Iterate, Don't Quit If a prompt doesn't work, don't give up. Refine it. Adjust it. Try again. Every "failure" is a learning opportunity.

4. Study Others Look at prompts other people have shared. Join AI communities. Learn from people who are getting great results.

5. Experiment Fearlessly Try weird things. Test assumptions. Push boundaries. The best prompts often come from experimentation.

6. Measure Your Progress Track your time savings. Note the quality improvements. Celebrate your wins. Progress is motivating.

Real Example of Progression

Let me show you what this journey looks like in practice.

Week 1: Maya, a 22-year-old marketing student, writes her first prompt: "Help me write a social media post." She gets a generic result that's not useful.

Week 3: Maya tries roleplay prompting: "You are a social media manager for a fashion brand. Write an Instagram caption for a new product launch." Much better. She's starting to see the power of specificity.

Week 6: Maya combines techniques: "You are a social media manager for a sustainable fashion brand targeting Gen Z. Here are three captions I've written that performed well Now write 5 more captions in the same style for our new collection. Explain why each caption would resonate with our audience." The results are excellent. She barely needs to edit them.

Week 10: Maya has built a library of prompt templates for every type of content she creates. She's working 3x faster than she was at the start. Her internship supervisor asks how she's producing so much high-quality work.

Week 12: Maya can't imagine working without AI. She's using it for research, content creation, brainstorming, and strategy. She's become the go-to person in her internship for "how to use AI effectively." She's already thinking about how to leverage this skill in her job search. That's the transformation. That's what 12 weeks of consistent practice looks like.

You're Building a Superpower That Will Set You Apart for the Next Decade

Here's what I want you to understand: by the end of these 12 weeks, you'll be in the top 1% of AI prompt engineers. Not because the skill is impossibly hard. But because most people never systematize their learning. They use AI casually, randomly, without intention. They never build the skill deliberately. You're different. You're following a plan. You're practicing consistently. You're building a skill that compounds over time. And here's the beautiful part: this skill is transferable across all AI tools. Whether it's ChatGPT, Claude, Bard, Midjourney, or whatever new tool launches next year, the principles are the same. You're learning how to communicate with AI, and that skill will serve you for the rest of your career. This skill will compound over time. The better you get at asking, the better every AI tool becomes. The better every AI tool becomes, the more you can accomplish. The more you can accomplish, the more opportunities open up for you. You're not just learning a tool. You're building a superpower. So here's your first step: commit to the 12-week plan. Put it in your calendar. Set reminders. Make it non-negotiable. 15-30 minutes a day. That's all it takes. In 12 weeks, you'll look back and think: This was the best investment I made all year. Let's get started. End of Chapter 4 You've got the tools. You've got the techniques. You've got the roadmap. In the next chapter, we're going to take everything you've learned and apply it to the thing that matters most: boosting your productivity and automating your workflow. You're about to learn how to work smarter, faster, and with less stress than you ever thought possible. Let's keep building.

CHAPTER

05

Boosting Productivity with AI Automation

CHAPTER

The Productivity Multiplier

Let me tell you about two people doing the exact same job. Sarah and Mike are both marketing coordinators at different companies. Same role. Same responsibilities. Same salary. They both manage social media, write blog posts, respond to customer emails, and create weekly reports for their managers. Here's the difference: Sarah works 50-hour weeks and still feels behind. She's constantly stressed, always rushing, never quite catching up. She takes work home on weekends. She's exhausted. Mike works 40-hour weeks and consistently exceeds his targets. He leaves the office on time. He has energy for his side projects. His manager keeps praising his output.

He just got promoted. What's the difference? Mike uses AI to automate 30% of his workload. That's it. That's the secret. He's not smarter than Sarah. He's not more talented. He doesn't work harder. He just works smarter. He's identified the repetitive, time-consuming tasks in his workflow and handed them off to AI. The time he saves? He reinvests it into the high-value work that actually moves the needle strategy, creativity, relationship-building. Sarah is still doing everything manually. She's working harder, not smarter. And she's burning out. This chapter is about making sure you become Mike, not Sarah.

The Math That Changes Everything

Let me show you some numbers that should get your attention. The average knowledge worker spends:

- 28% of their workweek managing email (that's 11 hours per week)
- 20% of their time searching for information or tracking down colleagues (8 hours per week)
- 15% of their time on repetitive administrative tasks (6 hours per week) Add it up. That's 25 hours per week — more than half of a typical work week—spent on tasks that could be partially or fully automated with AI. Now let's say you automate just 30% of those tasks. That's 7.5 hours per week. Over a year, that's 390 hours — nearly 10 full work weeks— that you get back. What could you do with an extra 10 weeks per year?
- Learn a new skill that makes you more valuable Take on high-impact projects that lead to

promotions

- Start a side business
- Actually, have a life outside of work
- Sleep more, stress less, enjoy your weekends

This isn't theoretical. This is real time that real people are saving right now by using AI to automate their workflows. And here's the beautiful part: you don't need to be a programmer. You don't need expensive software. You don't need to overhaul your entire system. You just need to know which tasks to automate and how to set up simple workflows using the tools you already have access to. That's what this chapter is about.

Working Smarter, Not Harder

Let me be clear about something: automation isn't about being lazy. It's not about cutting corners or doing less work. It's about redirecting your energy toward work that actually matters. Think about it this way: if you're spending two hours a day on email, that's two hours you're not spending on creative problem-solving, strategic thinking, or building relationships. Those are the things that actually advance your career. Those are the things that make you irreplaceable. Email? That's replaceable. Summarizing research? Replaceable. Drafting routine reports? Replaceable. Your judgment, your creativity, your ability to connect ideas and see the bigger picture? Irreplaceable. AI automation lets you offload the replaceable stuff so you can focus on what makes you valuable. Here's what I want you to understand: the people who win in the next decade won't be the ones who work the longest hours. They'll be the ones who automate the grunt work and focus their energy on high-leverage activities. You're about to learn how to become one of those people.

Identifying Tasks Worth Automating

Not every task should be automated. Some tasks require human judgment, creativity, or emotional intelligence. Some tasks are one-offs that take longer to automate than to just do manually. And some tasks are actually enjoyable—you might not want to automate them. So how do you know what to automate? I'm going to give you a simple framework. This is the same framework I use, and it's the same one I teach to professionals who want to optimize their workflows.

The Automation Decision Matrix

Ask yourself these four questions about any task: 1. Is it repetitive? Do you do this task more than once a week? If yes, it's a candidate for automation. 2. Is it time-consuming? Does it take more than 15 minutes each time you do it? If yes, automation could save you significant time. 3. Does it require minimal judgment? Is the task mostly following a template or process? If yes, AI can probably handle it. 4. Is it low-risk? If AI makes a mistake, is it easy to catch and fix? If yes, it's safe to automate. If a task checks three or more of these boxes, it's a strong candidate for automation. Let me show you what this looks like in practice.

Example 1: Email Responses

Is it repetitive? Yes—you probably answer similar questions multiple times per week. Is it time-consuming? Yes—even a simple email can take 5-10 minutes when you factor in thinking, drafting, and editing. Does it require minimal judgment? Mostly—many emails follow predictable patterns. Is it low-risk? Yes—you can review AI-generated emails before sending. Verdict: Strong candidate for automation.

Example 2: Strategic Planning

Is it repetitive? No—strategic decisions are unique to each situation. Is it time-consuming? Yes—but that's because it requires deep thinking. Does it require minimal judgment? No—this is all about judgment. Is it low-risk? No—bad strategic decisions have major consequences. Verdict: Don't automate. This is high-value human work.

Example 3: Social Media Captions

Is it repetitive? Yes—you need captions for every post. Is it time-consuming? Yes—writing engaging captions takes time. Does it require minimal judgment? Somewhat—there's a formula, but it needs your brand voice. Is it low-risk? Yes—you review before posting. Verdict: Good candidate for partial automation (AI drafts, you refine). See how this works? You're not automating everything. You're being strategic about where AI can save you time without sacrificing quality.

Your Personal Workflow Audit

Alright, let's make this practical. I want you to do a quick audit of your typical week. Grab a piece of paper (or open a note on your phone) and list out the tasks you do regularly. Don't overthink it—just brain dump everything you can think of. Here are some prompts to get you started: For students: Writing essays or papers

- Researching for assignments
- Taking notes in class Studying for exams
- Emailing professors
- Organizing research materials Creating presentations For freelancers:
- Responding to client emails
- Writing proposals
- Creating invoices
- Managing project timelines
- Drafting content (blogs, social posts, etc.)
- Researching competitors or trends
- Updating your portfolio for professionals: Managing email inbox
- Writing reports or summaries
- Scheduling meetings Creating presentations
- Researching industry trends
- Drafting internal communications Tracking project progress

Now, go through your list and apply the four-question framework to each task. Mark the ones that check three or more boxes. Those are your automation opportunities.

Start Small, Build Momentum

Here's a mistake I see people make all the time: they try to automate everything at once. They get overwhelmed, nothing sticks, and they give up. Don't do that. Instead, pick one task from your list—the one that's most repetitive and time-consuming—and focus on automating just that one thing this week.

Once you've got that working smoothly, pick another task. Then another. Small wins build momentum. Momentum builds confidence. Confidence leads to bigger changes. You're not trying to transform your entire workflow overnight. You're just trying to save 30 minutes this week. Then an hour next week. Then two hours the week after that. Before you know it, you've reclaimed 10+ hours per week. And it happened gradually, without stress, without overwhelm. That's the approach that actually works.

Real Example: The Freelancer Who Got Her Weekends Back

Let me tell you about Jessica, a 27-year-old freelance graphic designer. Jessica loved her work, but she was drowning in administrative tasks. Client emails, project updates, invoice reminders, social media posts—it never ended. She was working 60-hour weeks, and most of that time wasn't even spent designing. She was exhausted. She hadn't had a real weekend off in months. Then she did a workflow audit. She listed out every task she did in a typical week and applied the automation framework. Here's what she found: High automation potential:

- Client email responses (repetitive, time-consuming, low judgment)
- Social media captions (repetitive, time-consuming, low risk)
- Project status updates (repetitive, minimal judgment)
- Invoice follow-ups (repetitive, time-consuming, low risk, Low automation potential)
- Design work (requires creativity and judgment)
- Client consultations (requires emotional intelligence)
- Portfolio curation (requires strategic thinking)

Jessica decided to start with email responses. She created templates in ChatGPT for her most common email types: project inquiries, revision requests, timeline updates, payment reminders. Within a week, her email time dropped from 10 hours per week to 3 hours. Then she tackled social media. She used ChatGPT to generate caption drafts for her design posts. She'd review and tweak them, but the heavy lifting was done. Social media time: from 5 hours per week to 1.5 hours. Within a month, Jessica had automated about 12 hours of work per week. She was working 48-hour weeks instead of 60. She had her weekends back. She was less stressed, more creative, and actually enjoying her work again. And here's the kicker: her income didn't drop. In fact, it increased, because she had more time to take on higher-paying design projects. That's the power of strategic automation.

Automating Email & Communication

Let's start with the biggest time-suck for most people: email. If you're like most professionals, you spend 2-3 hours per day managing your inbox. That's 10-15 hours per week. That's 500-750 hours per year. What if you could cut that in half? You can. And it's easier than you think.

The Email Automation Framework

Here's the system I use, and it works for students, freelancers, and professionals: Step 1: Categorize your emails Most emails fall into predictable categories:

- Routine inquiries (people asking for information)
- Follow-ups (checking in on previous conversations)
- Requests (asking you to do something)
- Updates (informing people of progress or changes)
- Networking (introductions, coffee chats, etc.)

Step 2: Create templates for each category You don't need to write every email from scratch. Most emails follow a pattern. Create a template, and let AI customize it for each situation. Step 3: Use AI to draft, then review and personalize AI handles the structure and basic content. You add the personal touches and make sure it sounds like you. Let me show you exactly how this works.

Real Example: The Professional Email Workflow

Let's say you're a marketing coordinator and you get a lot of emails asking about campaign timelines.

Old way (manual):

1. Read the email

2. Think about what to say

3. Draft a response

4. Edit for tone and clarity

5. Proofread 6. Send

Total time: 8-10 minutes per email. If you get 5 of these per day, that's 40-50 minutes. New way (AI-assisted): 1. Read the email 2. Open ChatGPT and paste this prompt: *"I received this email: [paste email]. Write a professional response that: Thanks, them for their inquiry

- Provides the requested timeline information: [insert details]
- Offers to answer any follow-up questions
- Keeps a friendly but professional tone
- Keeps it under 100 words"*
- Review the AI-generated response
- Make any personal tweaks
- Copy into your email and send

Total time: 2-3 minutes per email. That's a 70%-time savings. Over a week, you just saved 3-4 hours. Over a year? That's 150-200 hours.

Specific Email Templates You Can Use Today

Let me give you some ready-to-use prompts for common email scenarios. Copy these, customize them for your situation, and start saving time immediately. Template 1: Responding to a Project Inquiry *"I received this inquiry email: [paste email]. Write a professional response that:

- Thanks, them for reaching out Confirms my interest in the project

- Asks 2-3 clarifying questions about [scope/timeline/budget]
- Suggests a time to discuss further
- Tone: enthusiastic but professional
- Length: under 150 words"*

Template 2: Following Up on a Previous Email *"I sent this email a week ago: [paste original email]. Write a polite follow-up that:

- References the original email
- Gently reminds them of what I'm waiting for
- Offers to provide any additional information
- Suggests a specific next step
- Tone: friendly and patient, not pushy
- Length: under 100 words"*

Template 3: Declining a Request Politely *"I received this request: [paste email]. Write a polite decline that: Thanks, them for thinking of me

- Explains that I'm unable to take this on right now due to [reason]
- Suggests an alternative if possible (e.g., recommending someone else)
- Leaves the door open for future opportunities
- Tone: warm and appreciative

Length: under 120 words"*

Template 4: Requesting Information or Help *"I need to ask [person's name] for [specific request]. Write an email that:

- Briefly explains the context Clearly states what I need
- Explains why I'm asking them specifically

- Makes it easy for them to say yes (specific, reasonable request)
- Tone: respectful and appreciative
- Length: under 150 words"*

See the pattern? You're giving ChatGPT the context, the goal, the tone, and the constraints. It handles the drafting. You handle the final polish.

The Cover Letter That Actually Gets Read

Let's talk about cover letters, because this is where AI can save you massive amounts of time, especially if you're job hunting or freelancing. Writing a good cover letter from scratch takes 1-2 hours. Most people either spend that time and burn out, or they send generic letters that get ignored. AI gives you a third option: personalized, high-quality cover letters in 15-20 minutes. Here's the workflow: Step 1: Gather your information

- The job description
- Your relevant experience and skills
- 2-3 specific accomplishments that match the role

Step 2: Use this prompt: *"I'm applying for this position: [paste job description]. Here's my relevant background: [brief summary of experience and skills]. Write a cover letter that:

- Opens with a strong hook that shows I understand the company's needs
- Highlights 2-3 specific accomplishments that demonstrate I can do this job
- Shows enthusiasm for the role and company
- Ends with a clear call to action

- Tone: confident but not arrogant, professional

but personable Length: 250-300 words"*

Step 3: Review and personalize The AI will give you a solid draft. Your job is to:

- Add specific details that make it uniquely yours
- Adjust the tone to match your voice
- Make sure every claim is accurate
- Add any company-specific research you've done

Total time: 15-20 minutes for a personalized, compelling cover letter. Compare that to 1-2 hours of staring at a blank page, and you can see why this is a game-changer.

Real Example: The Student Who Landed

Three Internships

Meet David, a 21-year-old college junior studying computer science. David was applying for summer internships. He knew he needed to send out at least 20 applications to have a good shot. But writing 20 unique cover letters? That would take 20-40 hours. He didn't have that kind of time. So, he used the AI-assisted approach. For each application, he'd: 1. Read the job description carefully 2. Identify 2-3 key requirements 3. Match those to his own projects and experience 4. Use ChatGPT to draft a cover letter 5. Spend 10-15 minutes personalizing it He sent out 25 applications in one week. Total time: about 8 hours (instead of 30-40 hours). He got 8 interviews. He received 3 internship offers. David told me: "The AI didn't write my cover letters for me—it helped me write them faster.

Every letter was still mine. I just didn't have to start from a blank page every time." That's the key insight: AI doesn't replace your effort. It amplifies it.

Email Time Saved: 30-45 Minutes Per Day

Let's do the math on what we've covered so far. If you implement just the email automation strategies in this section: Routine email responses: save 20-30 minutes per day

- Follow-ups and requests: save 10-15 minutes

per day Cover letters and formal communications: save hours per application That's 30-45 minutes per day. Over a year, that's 125-190 hours — more than three full work weeks. What would you do with an extra three weeks per year?

Automating Research & Information Synthesis

Research is one of those tasks that feels productive but often isn't. You spend hours reading articles, taking notes, trying to make sense of scattered information. You open 20 browser tabs. You copy-paste quotes into a document. You try to remember where you saw that one statistic. It's exhausting. And it's slow. AI can change this completely.

The Old Way vs. The New Way

Old research workflow

1. Google your topic

2. Open 10-15 articles

3. Read each one (or skim frantically)

4. Take notes in a separate document

5. Try to synthesize the information

6. Realize you forgot to note the source for a key fact

7. Go back and search again

8. Repeat until you hate everything Total time: 3-5 hours for a decent research session.

New research workflow:

1. Define your research question clearly

2. Use ChatGPT to get an overview and key themes

3. Ask for specific sources or studies to investigate

4. Use AI to summarize long articles or papers

5. Use Notion AI to organize and synthesize your notes 6. Generate an outline based on your research Total time: 45 minutes to 1.5 hours for the same depth of research. That's a 70-80% time savings.

How to Use AI for Research (The Right Way)

Let me be clear about something: AI is not a replacement for primary sources. You still need to verify information. You still need to read the actual studies or articles for anything important. But AI can dramatically speed up the process of finding, filtering, and organizing information. Here's how to do it effectively:

Step 1: Start with a broad overview Instead of diving into random articles, start by asking ChatGPT for a structured overview. Example prompt: *"I'm researching [topic]. Give me: A brief overview of the current state of this field

- The 3-5 main perspectives or schools of thought
- Key terms and concepts I should understand

Suggested areas to investigate further

Keep it concise—bullet points are fine."* This gives you a mental map of the landscape. Now you know what you're looking for.

Step 2: Identify key sources Example prompt: "Based on that overview, what are the most influential studies, papers, or books on [specific aspect]? Give me 5-7 sources I should prioritize, with a one-sentence description of why each is important." Now you have a reading list. You're not randomly Googling—you're strategically targeting the most valuable sources. Step 3: Summarize and extract key points This is where AI really shines. Instead of reading a 30-page paper from start to finish, you can: Example prompt: *"Here's a research paper: [paste text or provide link]. Summarize the:

- Main argument or thesis
- Key findings or conclusions
- Methodology (briefly)
- Limitations or criticisms
- How this relates to [your specific research

question] Keep it under 300 words."* You still need to read the original source for anything you're going to cite or rely on heavily. But this summary helps you decide which papers are worth deep reading and which ones you can skim. Step 4: Synthesize across multiple sources Once you've gathered information from several sources, use AI to help you see patterns and connections. Example prompt: *"I've researched [topic] and found these key points from different sources: [paste your notes]. Help me:

- Identify common themes or patterns
- Highlight areas of disagreement or debate
- Suggest a logical structure for organizing this information
- Point out any gaps in my research"*

This is where AI acts like a research assistant, helping you make sense of everything you've collected.

Real Example: The Graduate Student Who Finished Her Thesis Early

Let me tell you about Maria, a 24-year-old graduate student working on her master's thesis. Maria's thesis required extensive literature review—she needed to read and synthesize dozens of academic papers. Her advisor estimated it would take her 6-8 months just to complete the research phase. Maria was stressed. She had a part-time job to pay rent. She didn't have 40 hours a week to dedicate to research. Then she discovered AI-assisted research.

Here's what she did:

Week 1: She used ChatGPT to map out the key themes in her field. Instead of randomly reading papers, she now had a clear structure: five main themes, each with 8-10 key papers to read.

Weeks 2-6: For each paper, she'd:

1. Use ChatGPT to generate a summary

2. Read the original paper, focusing on the sections most relevant to her thesis
3. Use Notion AI to organize her notes by theme
4. Ask ChatGPT to help her identify connections between papers

Week 7: She used ChatGPT to help her synthesize all her research into a coherent outline for her literature review chapter. Total research time: 7 weeks instead of 6-8 months. Maria told me: "I was skeptical at first. I thought using AI was somehow cheating. But then I realized—I'm still reading the papers. I'm still doing the thinking. AI is just helping me work more efficiently. It's like having a research assistant who never sleeps." She finished her thesis four months ahead of schedule. She graduated early. She got a job offer before most of her classmates even started their thesis research. That's the power of AI-assisted research.

Research Time Saved: From Hours to Minutes

Let's be specific about the time savings: Literature review for a research paper:

- Old way: 8-12 hours
- AI-assisted: 2-4 hours
- Time saved: 6-8 hours

Competitive analysis for a business project:

- Old way: 4-6 hours

AI-assisted: 1-2 hours

- Time saved: 3-4 hours

Background research for a blog post or article:

- Old way: 2-3 hours
- AI-assisted: 30-45 minutes
- Time saved: 1.5-2 hours

If you do research even once a week, you're saving 3-8 hours per week. That's 150-400 hours per year. That's not just time saved. That's time you can reinvest in higher-value work.

Accelerating Content Creation: Blogs, Social Media, and More

Content creation is one of the most time-consuming tasks for students, freelancers, and professionals. Whether you're writing blog posts, creating social media content, drafting newsletters, or putting together presentations, the process is slow: brainstorming, outlining, drafting, editing, formatting. AI can cut this time by 60-70% without sacrificing quality. Let me show you how.

The Content Creation Workflow (AI-Assisted)

Here's the system that content creators, marketers, and students are using to produce more content in less time:

Step 1: Ideation (5-10 minutes) Instead of staring at a blank page hoping for inspiration, use AI to generate ideas. Example prompt: *"I'm a [your role/niche] creating content for [your audience]. Generate 10 content ideas about [topic] that are:

- Specific and actionable
- Relevant to current trends

- Likely to engage my audience

For each idea, include a one-sentence description of the angle."* You'll get 10 ideas in 30 seconds. Pick the best one and move on.

Step 2: Outline (5-10 minutes) Example prompt: *"I'm writing a [blog post/social media thread/article] about [chosen topic]. Create an outline that:

- Starts with a strong hook
- Includes 3-5 main points
- Ends with a clear takeaway or call to action
- Is structured for [your platform/audience]"*

Now you have a roadmap. You're not figuring out structure as you write—you're just filling in the sections.

Step 3: Draft (15-30 minutes) Here's where you have options: Option A: AI drafts, you edit Use ChatGPT to generate a first draft based on your outline. Then you edit, refine, and add your personal voice. Option B: You draft, AI enhances Write the first draft yourself, then use AI to improve clarity, add examples, or strengthen weak sections. Most people find Option A faster, but Option B often produces content that feels more authentic.

Step 4: Polish (5-10 minutes) Use Grammarly to catch errors and improve clarity. Use ChatGPT to punch up your headline or opening paragraph. Total time: 30-60 minutes for a high-quality blog post or article. Compare that to 3-4 hours of traditional writing, and you can see why this is transformative.

Real Example: The Freelance Writer Who Tripled Her Income

Let me tell you about Alicia, a 29-year-old freelance writer. Alicia was good at her job, but she was stuck. She could write about 2-3 high-quality blog posts per week. At $200-300 per post, she was earning $1,600-2,400 per month. It was enough to survive, but not enough to thrive. She wanted to scale, but she was already working 40+ hours per week. She couldn't write any faster without burning out. Then she started using AI to accelerate her content creation process. Here's what changed: Before AI:

- Ideation: 30-45 minutes per post Outlining: 30 minutes
- Drafting: 2-3 hours
- Editing: 30-45 minutes

Total: 4-5 hours per post

After AI:

- Ideation: 10 minutes (AI generates ideas, she picks the best) Outlining: 10 minutes (AI creates structure)
- Drafting: 45 minutes (AI drafts, she refines and adds her voice)
- Editing: 15 minutes (Grammarly + final polish)
- Total: 1.5-2 hours per post

She went from 2-3 posts per week to 6-8 posts per week. Same quality. Same client satisfaction. Triple the output. Her income went from $1,600-2,400/month to $4,800-6,400/month. Within six months, she was earning more than she ever had as a full-time employee—and working fewer hours. Alicia told me: "AI didn't make me a better writer. It made me a faster writer. And in freelancing, speed is money."

Social Media Content: From Daily Stress to Weekly Batch

Social media is another massive time-suck. If you're a content creator, freelancer, or small business owner, you know the pressure: you need to post consistently, but creating content every single day is exhausting. AI changes the game. Instead of creating content daily, you batch-create a week's worth of content in one sitting. The Social Media Batch Workflow:

Step 1: Generate a week's worth of ideas (10 minutes) Example prompt: *"I'm a [your niche] posting on [platform]. Generate 7 content ideas for this week that:

- Mix educational, inspirational, and engaging content
- Are relevant to [current season/trend/event]
- Would resonate with [your audience]

For each idea, suggest a format (carousel, single image, video, text post, etc.)"*

Step 2: Draft captions for all posts (20-30 minutes) Example prompt (repeat for each post): *"Write a [platform] caption for this idea: [paste idea]. The caption should:

- Start with a hook that stops the scroll
- Deliver value in 3-5 sentences

End with a question or call to action

- Include relevant hashtags
- Tone: [your brand voice]

Length: [appropriate for platform]"*

Step 3: Create visuals (20-30 minutes) Use Canva AI to generate graphics or use DALL-E for custom images. With templates and AI assistance, you can create a week's worth of visuals in under 30 minutes. Total time: 1 hour for a week's worth of social media content. Compare that to 15-30 minutes per day (7-14 hours per week), and you've just saved 6-13 hours per week.

Content Creation Time Saved: 60-70% Reduction

Let's summarize the time savings: Blog post (1,000-1,500 words):

- Old way: 3-4 hours
- AI-assisted: 1-1.5 hours
- Time saved: 2-2.5 hours per post

Social media content (7 posts):

- Old way: 7-14 hours per week

AI-assisted: 1-2 hours per week

- Time saved: 6-12 hours per week

Newsletter or email campaign:

- Old way: 2-3 hours
- AI-assisted: 45 minutes to 1 hour
- Time saved: 1-2 hours

If you create content regularly, you're saving 10-20 hours per week. That's 500-1,000 hours per year. That's not just time saved. That's a whole new career's worth of time.

AI-Assisted Coding & Technical Tasks

You might be thinking: "I'm not a developer. This section doesn't apply to me." Hold on. Even if you're not a professional programmer, you probably encounter technical tasks: building a simple website, automating a spreadsheet, setting up a database, troubleshooting software issues. These tasks used to require either hiring someone or spending hours learning how to do it yourself. Not anymore. AI can now help you with technical tasks even if you have zero coding experience.

ChatGPT as Your Coding Tutor

Let's say you need to build a simple website for your portfolio or small business. In the old world, you had three options: 1. Hire a developer ($1,000-5,000) 2. Learn web development from scratch (100+ hours) 3. Use a website builder and accept the limitations Now you have a fourth option: use ChatGPT to guide you through building it yourself. Example workflow: Step 1: Describe what you want *"I want to build a simple portfolio website with:

- A homepage with my bio and photo
- A projects page showcasing 5 projects
- A contact form
- Clean, modern design

I have no coding experience. Walk me through this step-by-step."* ChatGPT will give you a roadmap: which tools to use, what order to do things in, and where to start. Step 2: Get specific code when you need it "Write the HTML code for a contact form with fields for name, email, and message. Include basic styling." ChatGPT will generate the code. You copy-paste it. It works. Step 3: Troubleshoot when something breaks "I'm getting this error: [paste error message]. Here's my code: [paste code]. What's wrong and how do I fix it?" ChatGPT will explain the problem and give you the solution. You're not becoming a professional developer. But you're able to complete technical tasks that used to be completely out of reach.

Real Example: The Student Who Built an App

Let me tell you about Kevin, a 20-year-old business major with zero coding experience. Kevin had an idea for a simple app: a study timer that used the Pomodoro Technique. He wanted to build it for himself and maybe share it with classmates. In the old world, Kevin would have had to:

- Take a coding course (months of learning)
- Hire a developer (thousands of dollars)
- Give up on the idea

Instead, Kevin used ChatGPT as his coding tutor. He started with: "I want to build a Pomodoro timer app. I've never coded before. Where do I start?" ChatGPT recommended he use HTML, CSS, and JavaScript (simple web technologies) and pointed him to free resources. Then Kevin asked: "Write the code for a basic Pomodoro timer with a 25-minute work session and a 5-minute break." ChatGPT generated the code. Kevin copy-pasted it into a file. It worked. Over the next two weeks, Kevin kept asking ChatGPT to add features: sound notifications, customizable time intervals, a task list. Each time, ChatGPT would generate the code and explain what it did. By the end of the month, Kevin had a fully functional Pomodoro timer app. He shared it with his classmates. Dozens of people started using it. Kevin told me: "I didn't become a programmer. But I learned enough to build something useful. And I did it in a month instead of a year."

GitHub Copilot: The Professional Developer's Secret Weapon

If you are a developer (or learning to become one), you need to know about GitHub Copilot. It's an AI coding assistant that integrates directly into your code editor. As you type, it suggests entire lines or blocks of code. It's like autocomplete on steroids. Professional developers are using Copilot to:

- Write boilerplate code 10x faster
- Debug issues in seconds instead of hours
- Learn new programming languages on the fly
- Reduce repetitive coding tasks

The result? Developers are 30-50% more productive. Here's what's important: Copilot doesn't replace developers. It makes them faster. You still need to understand what the code does. You still need to make architectural decisions. You still need to test and debug. But the grunt work—the repetitive, time-consuming parts of coding—gets automated.

Technical Tasks Time Saved: 40-60% Reduction

Let's quantify the time savings: Building a simple website:

- Old way: 20-40 hours (if learning from scratch)

AI-assisted: 5-10 hours

- Time saved: 15-30 hours

Debugging code:

- Old way: 1-3 hours per bug
- AI-assisted: 10-30 minutes per bug
- Time saved: 50-90% of debugging time

Writing boilerplate code: Old way: 2-4 hours

- AI-assisted: 20-40 minutes
- Time saved: 1.5-3.5 hours

Even if you only do technical tasks occasionally, the time savings add up fast.

Measuring Your Time Savings & ROI

Alright, we've covered a lot of automation strategies. You've seen the potential time savings. You're probably excited to get started. But here's the thing: if you don't measure your results, you won't stick with it. Humans are motivated by progress. We need to see that what we're doing is working. Otherwise, we drift back to old habits.

That's why this final section is so important. I'm going to show you how to track your time savings and calculate your ROI (return on investment) from AI automation. This isn't complicated. You don't need fancy software. You just need a simple system.

The Simple Time-Tracking System

Here's what you're going to do: Step 1: Establish your baseline Before you start automating, track how long tasks currently take you. For one week, keep a simple log:

- Task name Time spent
- Date

You can do this in a note on your phone, a spreadsheet, or even a piece of paper. Don't overthink it. At the end of the week, you'll have a clear picture of where your time is going. Step 2: Implement one automation at a time Pick one task from your list. Automate it using the strategies from this chapter. Step 3: Track the new time for the next week, track how long that same task takes with AI assistance. Step 4: Calculate your time savings Subtract the new time from the old time. That's your time saved per instance. Multiply by how often you do that task per week. That's your weekly time savings. Multiply by 52. That's your annual time savings. Example: Task: Writing client email responses old time: 10 minutes per email × 10 emails per week = 100 minutes per week new time (with AI): 3 minutes per email × 10 emails per week = 30 minutes per week Time saved: 70 minutes per week = 60 hours per year See how simple that is?

Calculating Your Financial ROI

Time savings are great, but let's talk about money. If you're a freelancer or professional, your time has a dollar value. If you're a student, the time you save can be used to earn money (part-time job, freelance work, etc.). Here's how to calculate your financial ROI:

Step 1: Determine your hourly rate If you're a freelancer, this is easy—you already know what you charge. If you're an employee, divide your annual salary by 2,080 (the number of work hours in a year). If you're a student, estimate what you could earn with a part-time job or freelance work (typically $15-25/hour).

Step 2: Multiply your time savings by your hourly rate Example: You save 10 hours per week through automation. Your hourly rate is $25. 10 hours × $25 = $250 per week $250 × 52 weeks = $13,000 per year That's the value of the time you're getting back.

Step 3: Subtract the cost of your tools Let's say you're paying for ChatGPT Plus ($20/month) and Grammarly Premium ($12/month). That's $384 per year. Your net ROI: $13,000 - $384 = $12,616 per year. That's a 3,200% return on investment. Even if you only save 3 hours per week at $15/hour, that's still $2,340 per year in value—a 600% ROI. The math is undeniable.

The Motivation Tracker

Here's a psychological trick that will help you stick with AI automation: Create a "wins" document. Every time AI saves you significant time or helps you accomplish something faster, write it down:

- Date
- Task
- Time saved
- How you used that extra time

Example entries: "March 15: Used ChatGPT to draft client proposal. Saved 2 hours. Used the time to work on a new project pitch." "March

18: Batch-created a week of social media content in 1 hour instead of 7. Saved 6 hours. Spent the time learning a new skill." "March 22: AI-assisted research for essay. Finished in 1.5 hours instead of 4. Saved 2.5 hours. Actually, got a full night's sleep." When you see your wins accumulating, you'll be motivated to keep going. You'll start looking for more tasks to automate. You'll become addicted to the feeling of working smarter. That's when automation becomes a habit, not just a technique.

Real Example: The Professional Who Tracked Everything

Let me tell you about Rachel, a 32-year-old project manager. Rachel was skeptical about AI automation. She'd heard the hype, but she wasn't sure it would actually work for her. So, she decided to run an experiment. For one month, she'd track everything:

- Time spent on tasks before automation
- Time spent after implementing AI assistance

Total time saved

- What she did with the extra time

Here's what she found: Week 1:

- Automated email responses: saved 3 hours
- Used the time to finally organize her project files

Week 2:

- Automated meeting notes and summaries:

saved 2.5 hours

- Used the time to have coffee with a colleague

she'd been meaning to connect with Week 3:

- Automated report generation: saved 4 hours
- Used the time to work on a strategic initiative she'd been putting off Week 4:
- Automated research for a presentation: saved 3 hours
- Used the time to actually leave work on time and

go to the gym Total time saved in one month: 12.5 hours But here's what really convinced Rachel: she got promoted. Her manager noticed that Rachel was consistently delivering high-quality work ahead of schedule. She was taking on strategic projects that others didn't have time for. She seemed less stressed and more engaged. Rachel told me: "I didn't tell my manager I was using AI. I just showed up with better results. The promotion came three months later. The salary increases more than paid for every AI tool I'm using." That's the real ROI: not just time saved, but opportunities created.

You're Not Just Saving Time—You're Creating Opportunities

Here's what I want you to understand: the time you save through automation isn't just "free time." It's opportunity time. It's time you can invest in:

- Learning new skills that make you more valuable
- Taking on high-impact projects that lead to promotions
- Starting a side business
- Building relationships Actually having a life outside of work

The people who win in the next decade won't be the ones who work the hardest.

They'll be the ones who work the smartest—who automate the grunt work and focus their energy on what actually matters. You're about to become one of those people. End of Chapter 5 You now know how to identify tasks worth automating, set up practical workflows, and measure your results. You've seen real examples of people who've transformed their productivity using these exact strategies. In the next chapter, we're going to zoom out and look at the bigger picture: how AI is reshaping the job market, what skills will matter most in the future, and how to position yourself to thrive in this new landscape. You're not just learning to work faster. You're learning to future-proof your career. Let's keep going.

CHAPTER

06

Future-Proofing Your Career

CHAPTER

The Future of Work is Being Written Right Now

Let me tell you what's happening in the job market while you're reading this book. A 24-year-old with no formal tech background just got hired as a "Prompt Engineer" at a Fortune 500 company. Salary: $95,000. Six months ago, this job didn't exist. A marketing coordinator who learned to use AI tools got promoted to "AI Marketing Strategist" with a 40% salary increase. She's doing the same work she was doing before—she just knows how to do it with AI. A freelance writer who added "AI-assisted content creation" to her LinkedIn profile is now charging 50% more per project and getting more clients than she can handle. Meanwhile, thousands of people who are ignoring AI are watching their job security erode. They're working harder, earning the same (or less), and wondering why they're falling behind. Here's the reality: the job market is being rewritten right now. Not in five years. Not "eventually." Right now. And you have a choice to make. You can wait and see what happens—watch from the sidelines while others position themselves for the opportunities that are emerging. Or you can act now, while the window is still open, and position yourself as someone who understands where the market is going. This chapter is about making sure you choose the second option.

The Window is Open (But It Won't Stay Open Forever)

Here's something most people don't understand about career transitions: there's a brief window when new skills are valuable but not yet common. Right now, AI literacy is in that window. Companies need people who can use AI tools effectively. But most of their workforce doesn't have these skills yet. So the people who do have them? They're getting promoted faster, hired more easily, and paid more. But this window won't last forever. In 2-3 years, AI literacy will be expected—it'll be like knowing how to use email or Microsoft Office. It won't be a differentiator anymore. It'll just be table stakes. Right now, though? It's a competitive advantage. The people who are learning AI skills today are positioning themselves to be the managers, team leads, and specialists of tomorrow. They're the ones who'll train everyone else when AI literacy becomes mandatory. You want to be in that first group. Not the second.

What This Chapter Will Do For You

I'm going to show you: 1. What jobs are emerging (and how to position yourself for them) 2. What skills will matter most (and why human skills are becoming more valuable, not less) 3. How to build a personal brand that signals you're ahead of the curve 4. How to negotiate better pay using your AI competency as leverage By the end of this chapter, you'll have a clear roadmap for positioning yourself strategically in a rapidly changing job market. You're not just learning to use AI tools. You're learning to future-proof your career. Let's get started.

Emerging Roles Industries Shaped by AI

The job market is creating entirely new categories of work. Some of these roles didn't exist two years ago. Some are evolving so fast that job descriptions are being rewritten every few months. Here's what you need to know: these aren't just jobs for computer scientists or engineers. Many of them are accessible to anyone willing to learn. Let me show you what's out there.

The New Job Categories

1. Prompt Engineer What they do: Design and optimize prompts to get the best results from AI systems. They understand how to communicate with AI to produce high-quality outputs for specific use cases. Who's hiring: Tech companies, marketing agencies, content studios, consulting firms, any company using AI at scale. Salary range: $75,000 - $135,000 (entry to mid-level) Skills needed:

- Strong writing and communication skills
- Understanding of AI capabilities and limitations
- Domain expertise (marketing, legal, technical writing, etc.)
- Analytical thinking

Entry path: You don't need a computer science degree. You need to demonstrate that you can craft effective prompts and understand how to get consistent, high-quality results from AI tools. Build a portfolio of before-and-after examples showing how your prompts improved outputs. Real example: Sarah was a copywriter earning $50,000/year. She spent three months mastering prompt engineering and documenting her process. She applied for a Prompt Engineer role at a marketing tech company. They hired her at $85,000 because she could demonstrate real results. Within a year, she was earning $105,000.

2. AI Training Specialist / AI Trainer What they do: Help train AI systems by providing feedback, labelling data, and teaching AI to understand context, tone, and nuance in specific domains. Who's hiring: AI companies, tech startups, research labs, companies building custom AI solutions. Salary range: $45,000 - $80,000 (depending on specialization) Skills needed:

- Attention to detail
- Domain expertise (language, visual arts, specific industries)
- Ability to follow guidelines and provide consistent feedback
- Understanding of how AI learns

Entry path: Many companies hire AI trainers with no technical background. They're looking for people who understand language, context, and quality. Start with platforms like Scale AI, Appen, or Label box to gain experience, then move to full-time roles. Real example: Marcus was a recent college grad with an English degree, struggling to find work. He started doing AI training work part-time ($20/hour) while job hunting. After six months, he had enough experience to apply for a full-time AI Training Specialist role at a language AI company. Starting salary: $62,000. He's now training AI systems to understand literary analysis and creative writing.

3. AI Product Specialist / AI Solutions Consultant What they do: Help companies understand how to implement AI tools in their workflows. They're the bridge between technical AI capabilities and business needs. Who's hiring: AI software companies, consulting firms, enterprise tech companies, agencies. Salary range: $65,000 - $120,000 Skills needed:

- Understanding of AI tools and their applications
- Business acumen and problem-solving
- Communication skills (explaining technical

concepts to non-technical people) Project management

Entry path: This role is perfect for people with industry experience who add AI knowledge. If you've worked in marketing, sales, operations, or customer success, you can transition into this role by demonstrating AI

competency in your current field. Real example: Jennifer worked in customer success at a SaaS company ($58,000/year). She started using AI tools to improve her workflow and shared her results with her team. When her company started exploring AI solutions, she positioned herself as the internal expert. Six months later, she transitioned to an "AI Solutions Consultant" role at an AI software company. New salary: $95,000.

4. AI Content Strategist / AI-Assisted Content Creator What they do: Create content using AI tools, but with strategic oversight and human refinement. They understand how to use AI to scale content production while maintaining quality and brand voice. Who's hiring:

Marketing agencies, media companies, content studios, e-commerce brands, SaaS companies. Salary range: $55,000 - $95,000 Skills needed:

- Content creation and editing
- Understanding of AI content tools
- Brand voice and strategy
- SEO and content marketing knowledge

Entry path: If you're already creating content (writing, social media, video scripts, etc.), add AI tools to your workflow and document the results. Show that you can produce more content, faster, without sacrificing quality. Real example: David was a freelance content writer earning about $3,000/month. He learned to use AI tools to speed up his research and drafting process. He rebranded as an "AI-Assisted Content Strategist" and started pitching agencies. Within three months, he had two retainer clients paying him $4,500/month each. He's now earning $9,000/month working fewer hours than before.

5. AI Workflow Automation Specialist What they do: Help companies identify processes that can be automated with AI and implement those solutions. They're process optimization experts who use AI as their primary tool. Who's hiring: Operations teams, consulting firms, startups, any company looking to improve efficiency. Salary range: $60,000 - $110,000 Skills needed:

- Process mapping and analysis Understanding of AI automation tools
- Problem-solving and systems thinking
- Project management

Entry path: Start by automating workflows in your current role. Document the time savings and efficiency gains. Build case studies showing before-and-after metrics. This role is accessible to anyone with operations, project management, or business analysis experience. Real example: Priya worked in operations at a mid-sized company ($52,000/year). She used AI tools to automate several manual processes in her department, saving the team 15+ hours per week. She documented everything and presented it to leadership. They created a new role for her: "Workflow Automation Specialist" at $72,000. She now helps other departments implement AI automation.

6. AI Ethics Safety Specialist What they do: Ensure AI systems are being used responsibly, identify potential biases or risks, and develop guidelines for ethical AI use. Who's hiring: Tech companies, government agencies, consulting firms, large enterprises implementing AI. Salary range: $70,000 - $130,000 Skills needed:

- Critical thinking and ethical reasoning
- Understanding of AI capabilities and limitations
- Research and analysis skills
- Communication and policy development

Entry path: This role often attracts people with backgrounds in philosophy, law, social sciences, or policy. You don't need to be a programmer—you need to understand the societal implications of AI and how to create frameworks for responsible use. Real example: Alex studied philosophy in college and worked in nonprofit advocacy ($45,000/year). As AI became more prominent, he started writing about AI ethics and safety. He built a portfolio of thoughtful analysis and applied to AI companies looking for ethics specialists. He's now an AI Ethics Researcher at a major tech company earning $95,000.

Industries Being Transformed (Where the Opportunities Are)

It's not just about new job titles. Entire industries are being reshaped by AI, creating opportunities for people who understand how to work with these tools. Marketing Advertising:

- AI-powered personalization
- Automated content creation and optimization
- Predictive analytics for campaign performance
- Chatbots and customer engagement

Opportunities: Marketing roles that incorporate AI are seeing 25-40% salary premiums compared to traditional marketing roles. Healthcare:

- AI-assisted diagnostics
- Patient data analysis
- Administrative automation
- Personalized treatment planning

Opportunities: Healthcare administrators and coordinators who understand AI tools are in high demand. Non-clinical roles are opening up for people who can bridge the gap between medical professionals and AI systems. Education:

- Personalized learning platforms AI tutoring and assessment
- Curriculum development using AI insights
- Administrative automation

Opportunities: Educators who can design AI-enhanced learning experiences are becoming curriculum specialists and instructional designers at higher pay grades. Finance:

- Automated financial analysis
- Risk assessment and fraud detection
- Customer service automation
- Investment research and insights

Opportunities: Financial analysts and advisors who use AI tools are handling larger portfolios and earning higher commissions. Creative Industries:

- AI-assisted design and video production
- Music and audio generation
- Game development and 3D modelling
- Advertising creative development

Opportunities: Creatives who use AI to amplify their output are taking on more clients and charging premium rates for faster turnaround.

The Pattern You Need to See

Look at all these roles and industries. Notice the pattern? None of these jobs require you to build AI systems. They require you to use AI systems effectively. You don't need to be a machine learning engineer. You don't need a computer science degree. You don't need to understand the math behind neural networks. You just need to:

1. Understand what AI can do
2. Know how to use AI tools effectively

3. Apply AI to solve real problems in your field

4. Communicate the value you're creating That's it. That's the skillset that's opening up six-figure opportunities for people with no technical background.

How to Position Yourself for These Roles

Here's your action plan:

Step 1: Pick one emerging role that aligns with your background Don't try to pursue all of them. Pick the one that makes the most sense given your current experience and interests. If you're a writer or marketer fi AI Content

Strategist or Prompt Engineer fi

- If you're in operations or project management AI Workflow Automation Specialist
- If you're in customer-facing roles AI Product Specialist, If you have domain expertise in any field of AI Trainer in that domain

Step 2: Build demonstrable competency Start using AI tools in your current work. Document your results:

- Time saved Quality improvements
- New capabilities you've unlocked
- Problems you've solved

Create a portfolio of before-and-after examples.

Step 3: Update your professional presence Add AI skills to your LinkedIn profile. Share examples of your work. Write posts about what you're learning. Make it visible that you're ahead of the curve.

Step 4: Start applying or pitching Don't wait until you feel "ready." If you can demonstrate real results with AI tools, you're qualified. Apply for roles. Pitch clients. Have conversations. The market is moving fast. The people who act now will have a 2–3-year head start on everyone else.

Essential Skills: Technical vs. Human

Here's a question I get all the time: "If AI can do so much, what skills should I actually focus on developing?" Great question. And the answer might surprise you. The skills that will matter most in an AI-powered world are the ones AI can't do. Let me explain.

What AI is Really Good At

AI excels at:

- Processing large amounts of information quickly
- Identifying patterns in data
- Generating content based on patterns it's learned
- Following instructions and templates
- Performing repetitive tasks consistently

Analyzing and summarizing text

These are valuable capabilities. But they're also becoming commoditized. If AI can do it, it's not a differentiator for you.

What AI Can't Do (And Probably Never Will)

Here's what AI struggles with—and what makes you irreplaceable: 1. Emotional Intelligence AI can't read a room. It can't sense when someone is frustrated, excited, or holding back. It can't build genuine relationships or navigate complex interpersonal dynamics. Why this matters: As AI handles more routine work, the ability to connect with people, build trust, and navigate human emotions becomes more valuable, not less. How to develop it:

- Practice active listening (really hearing what people are saying, not just waiting to respond)
- Pay attention to non-verbal cues in conversations
- Seek feedback on how you come across to others
- Put yourself in situations that require empathy and relationship-building Real example: Two sales reps use the same AI tools to research prospects and draft emails. One closes 3x more deals than the other. Why? The successful one uses AI for research and drafting, but she builds relationships through genuine conversations, active listening, and emotional attunement. AI handles the prep work. She handles the human connection. 2. Creative Problem-Solving AI can generate ideas based on patterns it's seen before. But it can't make intuitive leaps. It can't combine unrelated concepts in novel ways. It can't look at a problem and say, "What if we approached this completely differently?" Why this matters: The problems worth solving are the ones that don't have obvious solutions. That's where human creativity becomes invaluable. How to develop it:
- Expose yourself to diverse fields and ideas (read widely, explore different industries)
- Practice asking "What if?" and "Why not?" questions
- Work on problems that don't have clear answers

- Collaborate with people who think differently than you

Real example: A marketing team uses AI to generate campaign ideas. They get 50 solid, conventional ideas. Then a junior team member says, "What if we did the opposite of what everyone in our industry does?" That insight—which came from creative thinking, not AI—leads to their most successful campaign ever. 3. Strategic Thinking AI can analyse data and identify trends. But it can't make judgment calls about what matters most. It can't weigh competing priorities. It can't decide which opportunities to pursue and which to ignore. Why this matters: Strategy is about making choices with incomplete information. It's about understanding context, anticipating second-order effects, and making bets on the future. That's human work. How to develop it:

- Practice thinking several steps ahead (if we do X, what happens next?)
- Study case studies of strategic decisions (both successes and failures)
- Take on projects that require prioritization and trade-offs
- Learn to ask "What's the goal?" before jumping to solutions Real example: A startup founder uses AI to analyse market data and generate business ideas. The AI suggests 20 viable business models. But the founder has to decide which one to pursue based on her understanding of the market, her team's strengths, and her vision for the company. That's strategic thinking. AI can inform the decision, but it can't make it. 4. Leadership Influence AI can't inspire people. It can't rally a team around a vision. It can't navigate organizational politics or build coalitions. It can't make people want to follow. Why this matters: As AI handles more execution work, the ability to

lead, motivate, and influence becomes the primary differentiator between individual contributors and leaders. How to develop it:

- Take on leadership roles (even small ones—lead a project, organize an event)
- Practice communicating vision and purpose, not just tasks
- Learn to give feedback that motivates rather than deflates
- Study great leaders and understand what makes them effective Real example: Two managers have the same AI tools to track projects and communicate with their teams. One team is engaged, productive, and loyal. The other has high turnover and low morale. The difference? Leadership. The effective manager uses AI for logistics but leads with vision, empathy, and inspiration. 5. Ethical Judgment AI can follow rules, but it can't make ethical judgments in complex situations.

It can't weigh competing values. It can't decide what's right when there's no clear answer. Why this matters: As AI becomes more powerful, the ethical questions become more important. Someone needs to make judgment calls about how AI should be used. That's human work. How to develop it: Engage with ethical dilemmas (read case

studies, discuss with others)

- Practice articulating your values and reasoning
- Consider second-order effects of decisions (who

benefits? who's harmed?)

- Develop a framework for making difficult choices

Real example: A company is deciding whether to use AI to screen job applicants. The AI is efficient, but it might perpetuate historical biases. Someone needs to weigh the trade-offs: efficiency vs. fairness, speed vs. equity. That's an ethical judgment that requires human wisdom, not just data analysis.

The Paradox: AI Makes Human Skills More Valuable

Here's what's counterintuitive: as AI gets better at technical tasks, human skills become more valuable, not less. Think about it this way: When everyone has access to the same AI tools, what differentiates you?

- Your ability to connect with people
- Your creative insights
- Your strategic judgment
- Your leadership presence
- Your ethical reasoning

These are the skills that can't be automated. And they're the skills that will determine who advances and who stagnates.

Your Skill Development Strategy

Here's how to think about skill development in an AI-powered world: Use AI to amplify your technical skills: Let AI handle research, drafting, data analysis,

routine tasks

- Use the time you save to develop deeper expertise

- Focus on understanding concepts, not memorizing information
  Invest heavily in human skills: Emotional intelligence
- Creative problem-solving
- Strategic thinking

Leadership and communication

- Ethical reasoning

Combine both: The most valuable professionals are the ones who can use AI tools effectively AND bring strong human skills to the table. You're not competing with AI. You're partnering with it. And the people who understand this will have a massive advantage over those who don't.

Building Your AI-Forward Personal Brand

Let me tell you about two people with identical skills. Both are 26-year-old marketing coordinators. Both use AI tools daily. Both are getting great results—faster content creation, better campaign performance, more efficient workflows. One of them gets recruited for a senior role at a tech company with a 50% salary increase. The other stays in their current role, unnoticed. What's the difference? The first person made their AI competency visible. The second person kept it to themselves. Here's the reality: it's not enough to be good at using AI. You need to signal that you're good at it. This section is about building a personal brand that positions you as someone who's ahead of the curve—someone who understands where the market is going and has the skills to thrive in it.

Why Personal Branding Matters Now

In a rapidly changing job market, visibility is currency. When companies are looking for people who understand AI, they're not just posting job listings and waiting for applications. They're searching LinkedIn for people who are already talking about AI. They're looking at portfolios. They're paying attention to who's demonstrating competency publicly. If you're using AI tools but nobody knows it, you're missing opportunities. If you're using AI tools and making it visible, opportunities come to you.

The Three Pillars of an AI-Forward Personal Brand

Pillar 1: Demonstrate Competency Don't just say you use AI tools. Show what you've accomplished with them. How to do this: On LinkedIn:

- Share before-and-after examples of projects you've completed with AI assistance
- Post about specific problems you've solved using AI tools
- Write short case studies showing your process

and results Example post: "I used to spend 6 hours per week on client reporting. Now it takes 45 minutes. Here's how I automated the process using ChatGPT and Notion AI: [brief explanation]. Time saved: 5+ hours per week. Quality: actually, improved because I'm catching insights I used to miss." In your portfolio:

- Create a dedicated section for AI-assisted projects
- Include metrics (time saved, quality improvements, new capabilities)

- Explain your process (what tools you used and why) In conversations:
- When discussing your work, mention how you use AI tools
- Share specific examples of results you've achieved
- Offer to help others learn (this positions you as an expert) Pillar 2: Share Your Learning Journey You don't need to be an expert to build a personal brand around AI. You just need to be learning publicly. How to do this: Document what you're learning:
- "I just discovered this ChatGPT prompt technique that improved my results by 50%..."
- "Here's what I learned from experimenting with AI image generation this week..."
- "I tried using AI for [task] and here's what worked (and what didn't)..." Share useful resources:
- Tools you've discovered
- Tutorials that helped you
- Articles or videos that changed your understanding Ask questions publicly:
- "Has anyone used AI for [specific task]? Looking for recommendations..."
- "What's your favorite AI tool for [use case]?"

This does two things: 1. It positions you as someone actively engaged with AI 2. It builds your network of people interested in the same topics Pillar 3: Position Yourself as a Bridge The most valuable people in any transition are the ones who can translate between the old world and the new world. You don't need to be the most technical person. You need to be the person who can explain AI to non-technical people and help them see how it applies to their work. How to do this: Write for your industry:

- "How [your profession] can use AI to [specific

benefit]"

- "5 AI tools every [your role] should know about"
- "What I learned from using AI in [your field] for 3

months" Offer to help colleagues:

- Run a lunch-and-learn session at your company
- Create a simple guide for your team
- Mentor someone who's just getting started with

AI Speak at events or on panels:

- Industry meetups
- Virtual webinars

Podcast interviews

You don't need a huge audience. You just need to be visible to the right people—hiring managers, potential clients, industry leaders.

LinkedIn Optimization: The Practical Checklist

LinkedIn is where most professional opportunities happen. Here's how to optimize your profile to signal AI competency: 1. Update your headline Before: "Marketing Coordinator at XYZ Company" After: "Marketing Coordinator | AI-Powered Content Strategy | Helping brands scale content production" 2. Add AI skills to your skills section Add these (if relevant):

- Prompt Engineering

AI-Assisted Content Creation

- ChatGPT
- AI Workflow Automation

AI Tools Applications

Ask colleagues to endorse these skills. 3. Rewrite your "About" section Include a paragraph about how you use AI in your work. Example: "I specialize in content marketing with a focus on AI-powered workflows. Over the past year, I've integrated AI tools into every stage of content creation—from research and ideation to drafting and optimization. This approach has allowed me to triple content output while maintaining quality and reducing production time by 60%. I'm passionate about helping teams leverage AI to work smarter, not harder." 4. Showcase AI projects in your experience section For each role, include bullet points about AI-related accomplishments: Example:

- "Implemented AI-assisted content workflow,

increasing team output by 150% while reducing production time by 40%" "Developed prompt engineering framework for

consistent brand voice across AI-generated content"

- "Trained team of 5 on AI tools, resulting in

department-wide efficiency gains of 25+ hours per week" 5. Post regularly (2-3 times per week) Share:

- Quick wins with AI tools
- Lessons learned

- Useful resources
- Industry insights

You don't need to write long posts. Short, valuable updates work great. 6. Engage with AI-related content Comment on posts about AI in your industry. Share your perspective. Ask questions. This increases your visibility and positions you as engaged with the topic.

Real Example: The Career Change That

Started With LinkedIn

Let me tell you about Megan, a 28-year-old customer success manager. Megan had been using AI tools for about six months. She was getting great results—faster response times, better customer insights, more efficient

workflows. But she hadn't told anyone outside her immediate team. Then she decided to start posting on LinkedIn. Week 1: She shared a simple post about how she used ChatGPT to analyse customer feedback and identify patterns. 47 likes, 8 comments. Week 2: She posted a before-and-after example of an email she drafted with AI assistance. 93 likes, 15 comments, 2 connection requests from recruiters. Week 3: She wrote a short guide: "5 AI prompts every customer success manager should know." 200+ likes, 30+ comments, 12 connection requests. Week 6: A recruiter reached out about an "AI Customer Experience Specialist" role at a SaaS company. The role didn't exist three months ago. Salary: $85,000 (she was making $62,000). Week 8: She interviewed. They asked about her AI experience. She walked them through her LinkedIn posts, showing real examples of how she'd used AI to improve customer outcomes.

Week 10: She got the offer. $90,000 base + equity. Megan told me: "I was doing the same work before I started posting. But nobody knew about it. Once I made it visible, opportunities started coming to me. I didn't even apply for this job—they found me." That's the power of personal branding.

You Don't Need to Be an Influencer

Let me be clear: you don't need thousands of followers. You don't need to become a "thought leader." You don't need to post every day. You just need to be visible enough that when someone searches for "[your profession] + AI" or "[your skill] + AI tools," your name comes up. You just need to signal: "I'm someone who understands where this is going, and I'm already there." That's enough to open doors.

Negotiating Better Pay: The AI Advantage

Let's talk about money. You've learned AI skills. You're using them to produce better results faster. You're saving your company time and money. Now it's time to get paid for that value. This section is about how to translate your AI competency into higher compensation—whether you're negotiating a raise, interviewing for a new role, or setting rates as a freelancer.

The Data: AI Skills Command Premium Pay

Let me show you some numbers: According to recent salary surveys:

- Marketing professionals with AI skills earn

25-35% more than those without

- Content creators who use AI tools charge 30-50% higher rates
- Operations roles that include AI automation pay 20-40% above traditional ops roles
- Entry-level "AI-adjacent" roles (Prompt Engineer, AI Trainer, etc.) start 15-30% higher than comparable entry-level positions Real examples:
- Traditional Marketing Coordinator: $45,000-55,000
- AI-Powered Marketing Coordinator: $60,000-75,000
- Traditional Content Writer: $50,000-65,000
- AI Content Strategist: $70,000-90,000
- Traditional Operations Analyst: $55,000-70,000
- AI Workflow Automation Specialist: $75,000-95,000 The pattern is clear: AI competency translates directly to higher pay. But here's the thing: you don't get paid more just because you have the skills. You get paid more because you can articulate the value you're creating.

How to Quantify Your Value

Before you negotiate, you need to know your numbers.

Step 1: Calculate time savings How much time are you saving (yourself or your team) by using AI tools? Example:

- You automated a reporting process that used to take 4 hours per week
- That's 208 hours per year
- At your current salary of $50,000/year, your time

is worth about $24/hour Time savings value: 208 hours × $24 = $4,992 per year

Step 2: Calculate productivity gains How much more are you producing with AI assistance? Example:

- You used to create 2 blog posts per week
- With AI tools, you now create 5 blog posts per week
- That's a 150% increase in output

If each blog post generates $500 in value

(traffic, leads, etc.), you're creating an additional $78,000 in value per year

Step 3: Calculate quality improvements Has AI helped you improve the quality of your work in measurable ways? Example:

- Your AI-assisted content has 40% higher engagement rates
- Your AI-optimized campaigns have 25% better conversion rates
- Your AI-enhanced customer responses have improved satisfaction scores by 15% These improvements have real business value. Quantify them. Step 4: Add it up Now you have concrete numbers to bring to a negotiation:
- "I've saved the team 200+ hours this year through AI automation"
- "I've increased content output by 150% while maintaining quality"
- "My AI-enhanced campaigns are converting 25% better than our previous benchmarks" This isn't bragging. It's demonstrating value.

The Negotiation Framework

Whether you're asking for a raise, negotiating a job offer, or setting freelance rates, here's the framework: 1. Lead with value, not skills Don't say: "I've learned to use ChatGPT and other AI tools, so I think I deserve a raise." Do say: "Over the past six months, I've implemented AI tools that have increased my productivity by 150% and saved the team 10+ hours per week. I'd like to discuss adjusting my compensation to reflect the value I'm creating." 2. Use specific examples Don't say: "I'm using AI to work more efficiently." Do say: "I automated our client reporting process using AI, which reduced the time from 4 hours to 45 minutes per week. That's saving the company about $5,000 per year in labour costs, and the reports are actually more comprehensive now." 3. Position it as a win-win Don't say: "I'm doing more work, so I should be paid more." Do say: "I've found ways to create significantly more value for the company using AI tools. I'd like to discuss how we can structure my compensation to reflect this increased contribution." 4. Have a specific number in mind Don't say "I'd like a raise." Say "Based on the value I'm creating and market rates for AI-skilled professionals in this role, I'm looking for a salary adjustment to $X." Do your research. Know what people with your skills are earning.

Scripts for Different Scenarios

Scenario 1: Asking for a raise at your current job "I wanted to schedule time to discuss my compensation. Over the past [timeframe], I've integrated AI tools into my workflow, which has resulted in [specific results: time saved, productivity increase, quality improvements]. Based on market research, professionals with these

AI skills in similar roles are earning [salary range]. I'd like to discuss adjusting my salary to [specific number] to reflect the value I'm creating." Scenario 2: Negotiating a job offer "I'm excited about this opportunity. I noticed the salary range is $X-$Y. Given my demonstrated experience with AI tools and the results I've achieved—[specific examples]—I believe my skills align with the higher end of that range. Would you be open to an offer of /$$ [specific number]?" Scenario 3: Setting freelance rates "My rate is $[X] per [hour/project]. This reflects my use of AI tools to deliver higher quality work in less time. For example, [specific example of how AI enhances your work]. This means you get [benefit to client: faster turnaround, better results, more comprehensive deliverables] without paying a premium for it." Scenario 4: Asking for a promotion "I'd like to discuss my career path here. I've been using AI to expand my capabilities beyond my current role—[specific examples]. I'm now handling work that's typically done at the [next level] position. I'd like to explore formalizing this with a promotion to [title] and corresponding salary adjustment to $[number]."

Real Example: The 40% Raise

Let me tell you about James, a 25-year-old data analyst. James had been using AI tools for about eight months. He'd automated several reporting processes, improved the quality of his analysis, and was consistently delivering insights faster than his colleagues. But he was still earning $58,000—the same salary he started with two years ago. He decided it was time to negotiate. Here's what he did: Step 1: He documented his results

- Automated 3 major reporting processes (saving

12 hours per week)

- Improved analysis quality (his recommendations

led to a campaign that generated $200K in additional revenue)

- Trained 4 colleagues on AI tools (multiplying the

impact across the team) Step 2: He researched market rates

- Data analysts with AI skills in his city:

$75,000-95,000

- His current salary: $58,000

Gap: significant

Step 3: He scheduled a meeting with his manager He came prepared with:

- A one-page summary of his AI-driven results
- Market salary data
- A specific ask: $80,000 (a 38% increase)

Step 4: He made his case "Over the past eight months, I've integrated AI tools into my workflow in ways that have created significant value for the team. I've automated processes that save 12 hours per week, my AI-enhanced analysis contributed to a campaign that generated $200K in revenue, and I've trained four colleagues on these tools. Based on market research, data analysts with these AI skills are earning $ 75-95K. I'm asking for an adjustment to $80,000 to reflect the value I'm creating." The result: His manager agreed to $78,000—a 34% raise. James told me: "I was nervous to ask. But I had the numbers. I could show exactly what value I was creating. It wasn't about asking for more money—it was about getting paid fairly for the value I was already delivering."

What If They Say No?

Sometimes the answer is no. The company doesn't have budget. They're not ready to adjust compensation. They don't see the value the way you do. Here's what to do: 1. Ask what it would take "I understand budget is tight right now. What would I need to demonstrate over the next [3/6 months] to revisit this conversation?" Get specific criteria. Then meet them. 2. Negotiate non-salary benefits If they can't increase salary, ask for: Professional development budget (to invest in

more AI training)

- Flexible work arrangements
- Additional vacation time
- A title change that reflects your expanded

responsibilities 3. Set a timeline "I'd like to revisit this conversation in [3/6 months]. In the meantime, I'll continue documenting the value I'm creating with these AI tools." 4. Consider your options If your current employer won't compensate you fairly for the value you're creating, other employers will. Update your LinkedIn. Start having conversations. Explore opportunities. You're not stuck. You have valuable skills. The market wants what you have.

For Freelancers: Raising Your Rates

If you're a freelancer, the negotiation is simpler: you just raise your rates. Here's how: 1. Calculate your new rate If you're 2x more productive with AI tools, you can either: Charge the same rate and work half the hours

(better work-life balance)

- Charge 1.5x your old rate and work the same

hours (higher income) Some combination of both

2. Announce it to existing clients "Starting [date], my rates will be increasing to $[new rate]. This reflects my investment in AI tools that allow me to deliver higher quality work in less time. You'll continue to get the same great results—actually, even better—with faster turnaround times." Most clients will accept it. The ones who don't? They're not your ideal clients anyway. 3. Quote new rates to new clients Don't apologize for your rates. State them confidently: "My rate is $[X]. This includes my use of advanced AI tools that ensure you get exceptional quality and fast turnaround." Real example: Lisa was a freelance writer charging $0.10 per word ($100 for a 1,000-word article). With AI tools, she could research and draft articles 3x faster. She raised her rates to $0.15 per word. Some clients left. But she replaced them with new clients at the higher rate. Her income went from $4,000/month to $7,500/month while working fewer hours.

The Bottom Line

AI skills are valuable. The market knows it. Employers know it. Clients know it. The only question is: are you going to get paid for that value? You've invested time in learning these skills. You're creating measurable results. You're ahead of the curve. Now it's time to make sure your compensation reflects that. Don't wait for someone to notice. Make your case. Show your value. Ask for what you're worth. The people who do this will earn 25-50% more than those who don't—even though they're doing the same work. Be the person who asks. End of Chapter 6 You now understand how the job market is being reshaped by AI, what emerging roles exist, which human skills will matter most, how to build a personal brand that signals your competency, and how to negotiate better pay. You're not just learning to use AI tools. You're positioning yourself strategically for a future that's already here. In the next chapter, we're going to look at real people who've done exactly what we've been discussing—students, freelancers, career changers, and professionals who've used AI to transform their careers and their lives. You'll see yourself in their stories. And you'll see exactly what's possible when you take action. Let's keep going.

CHAPTER

07

Real-World Case Studies Success Stories

CHAPTER

See Yourself in These Stories

I need you to understand something before we dive into these case studies: These are not exceptional people. They're not geniuses. They don't have computer science degrees. They didn't have special connections or massive savings accounts. They weren't "naturally talented" with technology. They were just regular people—students stressed about money, professionals feeling stuck in their careers, freelancers working too many hours for too little pay, creatives burning out from the grind. The only thing that made them different was this: they decided to try. They didn't wait until they felt ready. They didn't wait for permission. They didn't wait until they understood everything about AI. They just started. They experimented. They made mistakes. They adjusted. They kept going. And within months—not years, months—their lives looked completely different. I'm sharing these stories because I want you to see yourself in them. I want you to recognize that the person in these case studies could be you six months from now. Different backgrounds. Different goals. Different industries. But the same pattern learn AI tools apply them strategically create measurable value get rewarded for it. That's it. That's the formula. You're about to meet five people who followed that formula. Their stories are different, but the outcome is the same: they're earning more, working smarter, and building careers they actually enjoy. Let's start with a college student who turned AI skills into a thriving freelance business while still in school.

Case Study 1: The Student Who Became a Freelancer

Meet Alex: The Broke College Junior

Alex was 20 years old, halfway through his junior year studying business at a state university, and he was broke. Not "I need to budget carefully" broke. Actually broke. He was working 15 hours a week at a campus coffee shop for $12/hour, which barely covered his share of rent and groceries. His student loans were piling up. He couldn't afford to go out with friends. He was stressed about money constantly. He'd tried to find better-paying work, but the options were limited: retail jobs that paid the same as the coffee shop, or unpaid internships that he couldn't afford to take because he needed income now. Alex told me: "I felt trapped. I needed money to survive, but the jobs I could get paid so little that I was just treading water. I couldn't save. I couldn't invest in my future. I was just... stuck." Then, in February of his junior year, a friend mentioned ChatGPT. Alex had heard about AI but assumed it was for tech people, not business majors like him. But he was desperate enough to try anything.

What Alex Did: From Zero to Freelance Writer in 90 Days

Month 1: Learning and Experimenting (February) Alex started simple. He signed up for ChatGPT (free version) and just... played with it. He asked it to help him with his homework. He used it to brainstorm essay topics. He had it summarize articles he needed to read for class. Within a week, he realized something: this thing could write. Not perfectly. But well, enough that with some editing, the output was actually good. He thought: "If I can use this to write my essays faster, could I use it to write for other people?" He spent the rest of February learning prompt engineering. He'd write prompts, evaluate the outputs, refine the prompts, repeat. He treated it like a part-time job: 1-2 hours every night after his coffee shop shift. He focused specifically on business writing—blog posts, LinkedIn articles, website copy—because that's what he understood. Month 2: Building a Portfolio and Landing First Clients (March) Alex needed a portfolio, but he had no professional writing samples. So, he created them. He used ChatGPT to help him write five sample blog posts on business topics: productivity tips for entrepreneurs, marketing strategies for small businesses, how to build a personal brand, etc. He didn't just copy-paste AI outputs. He used AI to draft, then he edited heavily, added his own insights, and polished until the posts were genuinely good. He published them on Medium (free platform). They weren't viral hits, but they looked professional. Then he created a simple one-page website using Carrd (free website builder) showcasing his "portfolio" and offering freelance writing services. His pitch was simple: "I write high-quality blog posts and website copy for small businesses. Fast turnaround, affordable rates." He started reaching out to small businesses on LinkedIn and through local business Facebook groups. His message: "Hi [name], I noticed you [specific observation about their business]. I'm a freelance writer specializing in [their industry]. I'd love to help you with content for your

blog/website. Here's my portfolio: [link]. Would you be open to a quick conversation?" He sent 50 messages. He got 3 responses. One turned into a paid project: a 1,500-word blog post for $75. It wasn't much. But it was proof of concept. Month 3: Scaling Up (April) Alex took that first client project seriously. He used ChatGPT to research the topic, outline the post, and draft the content. Then he spent hours editing, fact-checking, and making sure it was actually valuable. The client loved it. They hired him for three more posts. He asked for a testimonial. They gave him a glowing review. He updated his website with the testimonial and kept pitching. This time, he had social proof. By the end of April, he had four clients and was earning about $800/month from freelance writing—on top of his coffee shop job. He was working about 10 hours per week on freelance projects. That's $80/hour effective rate, compared to $12/hour at the coffee shop. He quit the coffee shop.

The Results: $3,200/Month by Graduation

By the end of his junior year (May), Alex was earning $1,200/month from freelance writing. Over the summer, he doubled down. He raised his rates (from $75 per post to $150 per post). He added more clients. He started offering package deals. By the time senior year started in September, he was earning $2,500/month. By graduation in May of the following year, he was earning $3,200/month—more than many of his classmates would earn in their first full-time jobs. And here's the beautiful part: he was working about 20 hours per week. He had time for classes, friends, and actually enjoying his last year of college. The numbers:

- Before AI: $12/hour at coffee shop = ~$720/month (15 hours/week)
- After AI (1 year later): $3,200/month freelance writing (~20 hours/week)
- Effective hourly rate: $160/hour
- Total earnings increase: 344%

What Alex Learned: The Key Insights

I asked Alex what he wished he'd known when he started. Here's what he told me:

1. "You don't need to be a great writer. You need to be a great editor." "I'm not a naturally talented writer. I'm decent, but not exceptional. What AI did was give me a starting point that was 70% of the way there. My job was to take it from 70% to 95%. That's way easier than starting from zero.

2. " 2. "Start before you're ready." "I had no portfolio, no experience, no credentials. I just started anyway. I created samples, I pitched clients, I figured it out as I went. If I'd waited until I felt 'ready,' I'd still be working at that coffee shop."

3. "Charge more than you think you should." "My first client paid me $75 for a post that took me 3 hours (including research and editing). That's $ 25/hour—better than the coffee shop, but not great. When I raised my rates to $150, I expected clients to say no. But they didn't. They just paid it. I was undervaluing myself because I didn't have confidence yet."

4. "AI is a tool, not a shortcut." "Some people think using AI is cheating. It's not. It's like using a calculator for math or a spell-checker for writing. The AI helps with the mechanical parts, but I still need to understand the topic, know what good writing looks like, and make strategic decisions. The value I provide is judgment and quality control, not just typing words."

Where Alex Is Now

Alex graduated debt-free (he used his freelance income to pay off his student loans early). He turned down several corporate job offers because his freelance business was more profitable and gave him more freedom. He's now 23, earning $5,000-6,000/month as a freelance writer, working 25-30 hours per week, and traveling while he works. He told me: "AI didn't just give me a side hustle. It gave me a completely different life trajectory. My classmates are working 50-hour weeks in corporate jobs they don't love. I'm working 25 hours a week, earning more than most of them, and I have complete control over my time. That's not luck. That's just knowing how to use the right tools."

Case Study 2: The Career Changer Who Learned AI

Meet Priya: The Burned-Out Teacher

Priya was 31 years old and exhausted. She'd been teaching high school English for seven years. She loved her students, but the job was grinding her down: 60-hour work weeks, endless grading, administrative bureaucracy, and a salary of $48,000 that hadn't kept pace with the cost of living. She wanted out. But she had no idea what else to do. She had a degree in English Literature—not exactly a hot commodity in the job market. She had no tech skills, no business experience, no "marketable" expertise beyond teaching. Every job posting she looked at required skills she didn't have: "3+ years of experience in marketing," "proficiency in data analysis," "familiarity with CRM systems." She felt stuck. She couldn't afford to go back to school. She couldn't afford to take an unpaid internship. She needed to keep earning while she figured out her next move. Priya told me: "I felt like I'd wasted my twenties. I had this degree that didn't translate to anything outside of teaching, and I was too old to start over from scratch. I was depressed and didn't see a way forward." Then she stumbled across an article about people using AI to change careers. She was skeptical, but desperate enough to try.

What Priya Did: From Teacher to Content Strategist in 8 Months

Months 1-2: Learning AI Tools and Identifying Transferable Skills (January-February) Priya started by signing up for ChatGPT and experimenting with it for her teaching work. She used it to generate discussion questions, create lesson plan outlines, and draft feedback on student essays. She realized: "I'm actually really good at this. I know how to ask the right questions to get useful outputs. I know how to evaluate quality. I know how to communicate clearly." Those were skills. Valuable skills. She started researching careers that valued those skills: content strategy, copywriting, instructional design, marketing. She decided to focus on content strategy because it combined her writing skills with strategic thinking—and it paid well ($60,000-90,000 for entry-level roles).

Months 3-4: Building New Skills and a Portfolio (March-April) Priya had a problem: she had no professional content strategy experience. So, she created it. She started a blog about education technology and teaching strategies. She used AI to help her research topics, outline posts, and draft content. She published one post per week. She also volunteered to help a local nonprofit with their content strategy—writing blog posts, managing their social media, creating email newsletters. She did it for free for two months to build real-world experience. She documented everything: the strategy she developed, the results (increased website traffic, higher email open rates), the tools she used. She created a simple portfolio website showcasing this work.

Months 5-6: Upskilling and Positioning (May-June) Priya knew she needed to understand marketing and analytics to be competitive for content strategy roles. She took two free online courses: Google Analytics and HubSpot Content Marketing. She completed them in about 20 hours total. She updated her LinkedIn profile: New headline: "Content Strategist | Education

Technology | Helping organizations communicate complex ideas clearly"

- New summary emphasizing her AI-enhanced

workflow and results from her nonprofit work Added skills: Content Strategy, SEO, ChatGPT,

AI-Assisted Writing, Google Analytics She started posting on LinkedIn about what she was learning. Short posts, 2-3 times per week. Nothing fancy—just sharing insights and lessons. Months 7-8: Job Search and Landing the Role (July-August) Priya started applying for Content Strategist and Content Marketing roles. She tailored every application. She used ChatGPT to help her customize cover letters for each company, but she added personal touches and specific research about each organization. Her pitch was simple: "I'm a career

changer with a unique background. I spent seven years teaching—which means I know how to communicate complex ideas clearly, understand audience needs, and create engaging content. I've spent the past six months building content strategy skills using AI tools to accelerate my learning. Here's what I've accomplished: [portfolio link]." She applied to 35 positions. She got 8 interviews. She received 2 offers. She accepted a Content Strategist role at an education technology company. Starting salary: $68,000. That's a 42% salary increase from teaching—and she was working 40-hour weeks instead of 60.

The Results: Career Transformation in 8 Months

The numbers:

- Before: High school teacher, $48,000/year, 60-hour weeks, burned out
- After: Content Strategist, $68,000/year, 40-hour weeks, energized
- Salary increase: $20,000/year (42%) Time to transition: 8 months
- Cost of transition: $0 (all free tools and courses) But the numbers don't tell the whole story. Priya told me: "The money is great, but what really changed is how I feel about my work. I'm not dreading Mondays anymore. I'm not exhausted every weekend. I actually enjoy what I do. That's worth more than the salary increase."

What Priya Learned: The Key Insights

1. "Your skills are more transferable than you think." "I thought my teaching experience was worthless outside of education. But the skills I used every day—clear communication, understanding audience needs, breaking down complex topics—those are exactly what content strategists do. I just needed to reframe them."

2. "You don't need years of experience. You need proof of competency." "I had zero professional content strategy experience. But I had a portfolio showing I could do the work. I had results from my nonprofit project. I had a blog demonstrating my thinking. That was enough. Employers care more about what you can do than how long you've been doing it."

3. "AI accelerates learning, but you still have to do the work." "AI helped me learn faster—I could research topics in minutes instead of hours, draft content quickly, get feedback on my ideas. But I still had to put in the hours. I still had to build real projects. AI didn't do it for me. It just made the process faster."

4. "Career changes are scary, but staying stuck is scarier." "I was terrified to leave teaching. It was stable, predictable, safe. But I was miserable. The scariest thing I did was decide to try something new. But looking back, staying in a job that was draining me would have been way scarier."

Where Priya Is Now

Priya has been in her Content Strategist role for 18 months. She got promoted to Senior Content Strategist after one year, with a salary increase to $82,000. She's now leading content strategy for her company's flagship product. She manages a small team. She's respected and valued. She told me: "I'm 33 now. If I'd stayed in teaching, I'd probably still be making $50,000 and counting down the years until retirement. Instead, I'm earning $ 8 2,000, working reasonable hours, and actually building a career I'm excited about. AI didn't hand me this career—but it made the transition possible."

Case Study 3: The Solo Business Owner Who Scaled

Meet Marcus: The Overwhelmed Freelancer

Marcus was 28 years old, running a one-person graphic design business, and he was drowning. He'd been freelancing for three years.

He was talented—his clients loved his work. But he was stuck in a cycle: he could only take on so many projects because he was doing everything himself. Design work. Client communication. Invoicing. Social media. Marketing. Project management. Revisions. More revisions. He was working 55-60 hours per week and earning about $4,500/month. That's roughly $18-20/hour—less than he'd make at many full-time jobs. He wanted to scale. He wanted to hire help. But he couldn't afford to hire anyone because his margins were too thin. Marcus told me: "I felt like I was running on a hamster wheel. I was working all the time, but I couldn't grow. Every time I took on a new client, I had to work more hours. There was no leverage. I was just trading time for money, and I was running out of time." He'd tried to optimize his workflow—better project management tools, templates, batching similar tasks—but he'd hit a ceiling. There were only so many hours in a week. Then he discovered AI automation.

What Marcus Did: From Solo Grind to Scalable Business in 6 Months

Month 1: Identifying Bottlenecks (January) Marcus did a time audit. He tracked every task he did for one week and categorized them: High-value work (requires his expertise):

- Design concepts and creative direction: 20 hours/week Client consultations and strategy: 5 hours/week

Low-value work (necessary but doesn't require his expertise):

- Client emails and communication: 8 hours/week
- Social media content creation: 6 hours/week
- Project updates and status reports: 4 hours/week

- Invoicing and administrative tasks: 3 hours/week

Research and inspiration gathering: 4 hours/week He was spending 25 hours per week—nearly half his time—on tasks that didn't require his design skills. That was the problem. And that's what he decided to automate.

Month 2: Automating Communication (February) Marcus started with email. He used ChatGPT to create templates for his most common email types:

- Project inquiry responses
- Revision request acknowledgments
- Timeline updates
- Payment reminders
- Project completion follow-ups

Instead of writing each email from scratch, he'd paste the template into ChatGPT, add context about the specific client/project, and get a customized email in 30 seconds. Time saved: Email time dropped from 8 hours/week to 2 hours/week. That's 6 hours per week—312 hours per year.

Month 3: Automating social media (March) Marcus needed to post regularly on Instagram and LinkedIn to attract clients, but creating content was eating up 6 hours per week. He implemented a batch-creation workflow: 1. Once per week, he'd use ChatGPT to generate 7 post ideas based on recent projects or design trends 2. He'd use ChatGPT to draft captions for each post 3. He'd use Canva AI to create graphics or mock-ups 4. He'd schedule everything using a free scheduling tool Time saved: Social media time dropped from 6 hours/week to 1.5 hours/week. That's 4.5 hours per week—234 hours per year.

Month 4: Automating Project Management (April) Marcus used ChatGPT to generate project status updates and client reports. Instead of manually writing updates, he'd input project details and milestones, and ChatGPT would generate professional updates. He also used AI to create project timelines and task lists for new projects, which used to take him 30-45 minutes per project. Time saved: 4 hours/week—208 hours per year.

Month 5: Automating Research and Inspiration (May) Marcus used ChatGPT to research design trends, gather inspiration, and analyse competitor work. What used to take 4 hours of browsing and note-taking now took 1 hour of targeted AI-assisted research. Time saved: 3 hours/week—156 hours per year. Total time saved across all automation: 17.5 hours per week—910 hours per year.

The Results: From $4,500/Month to $11,000/Month

With 17.5 extra hours per week, Marcus had a choice: work less or earn more. He chose both. He used 10 of those hours to take on more client work. He raised his rates by 30% (from an average of $1,500 per project to $2,000 per project) because he could deliver faster without sacrificing quality. He used the other 7.5 hours to actually have a life—exercise, hobbies, time with friends. The numbers after 6 months:

- Before automation: $4,500/month, 55-60 hours/week After automation: $11,000/month, 50 hours/week
- Revenue increase: 144%
- Hourly rate increase: from ~$18/hour to ~$55/hour but here's what really changed: Marcus could now afford to hire help. He brought on a part-time assistant ($15/hour, 10 hours/week) to

handle invoicing, client onboarding, and basic administrative tasks. He brought on a junior designer ($25/hour, as needed) to handle revisions and production work. Suddenly, he wasn't a solo freelancer anymore. He was running a small agency.

What Marcus Learned: The Key Insights

1. "You can't scale by working more hours. You scale by working smarter." "I thought the answer was to work harder, be more efficient, sleep less. But there's a ceiling to that. The breakthrough came when I realized I needed to offload the low-value work so I could focus on the high-value work. AI made that possible."

2. "Automation isn't about being lazy. It's about being strategic." "Some people hear 'automation' and think I'm cutting corners. But I'm not. The quality of my work actually improved because I'm spending more time on design and strategy, and less time on administrative BS. My clients are happier, not less happy."

3. "Small time savings compound into massive results." "Saving 30 minutes here, an hour there—it doesn't feel like much in the moment. But when you add it up over weeks and months, it's hundreds of hours. That's the difference between being stuck and being able to scale."

4. "Raising your rates is easier when you can deliver faster." "I was scared to raise my rates because I thought clients would leave. But when I could deliver the same quality in less time, clients were happy to pay more. Speed is valuable. AI gave me speed without sacrificing quality."

Where Marcus Is Now

Marcus is now 30. His business generates $15,000-18,000/month in revenue. After paying his assistant and occasional contractor help, he's netting about $12,000-14,000/month. He works 35-40 hours per week. He takes weekends off. He goes on vacation without his laptop. He told me: "Two years ago, I was working 60-hour weeks for $4,500/month and burning out. Now I'm working 35-40 hours for $ 1 2,000-14,000/month and actually enjoying my life. AI didn't build my business—I did. But AI made it possible to scale without killing myself."

Case Study 4: The Corporate Employee Who Got Promoted

Meet Jennifer: The Invisible High Performer

Jennifer was 26 years old, working as a Marketing Coordinator at a mid-sized tech company, and she was frustrated. She'd been in the role for two years. She was good at her job—maybe even great. She consistently hit her targets. Her manager praised her work. But she wasn't advancing. She watched colleagues get promoted while she stayed in the same role at the same salary: $52,000/year. She asked her manager about promotion opportunities. The answer was always the same: "You're doing great work, but we need to see you take on more strategic initiatives. Show us you can operate at the next level." The problem? She was already working 45-50 hours per week just keeping up with her current responsibilities. She didn't have time to take on "strategic initiatives." Jennifer told me: "I felt stuck. I was working hard, but I was stuck in execution mode—managing campaigns, writing copy, coordinating with vendors. I wanted to do strategic work, but I didn't have the bandwidth. It felt like a catch-22." Then she started using AI tools. Not because she was trying to get promoted—just because she wanted to work more efficiently. But efficiency created opportunity.

What Jennifer Did: From Coordinator to Strategist in 10 Months

Months 1-3: Automating Routine Work (January-March) Jennifer started small. She used ChatGPT to speed up her most time-consuming tasks: Email responses: She created templates for common scenarios (campaign updates, vendor coordination, internal requests). Time saved: 5 hours/week. Social media captions: She used ChatGPT to draft captions for the company's social accounts, then edited them to match brand voice. Time saved: 4 hours/week. Campaign reports: She used ChatGPT to help draft weekly campaign performance reports. She'd input the data, and ChatGPT would generate the narrative summary. Time saved: 3 hours/week. Total time saved: 12 hours per week. She didn't tell anyone she was using AI. She just quietly became more efficient.

Months 4-6: Reinvesting Time in Strategic Work (April-June) With 12 extra hours per week, Jennifer started doing the kind of work her manager said she needed to do to get promoted: Strategic initiative

#1: She analysed the company's content performance across all channels and identified patterns. She used ChatGPT to help synthesize the data and generate insights. She presented a comprehensive content strategy proposal to her manager. Her manager was impressed. They implemented several of her recommendations. Strategic initiative

#2: She noticed the company's email marketing was underperforming. She researched best practices (using AI to speed up research), ran A/B tests, and developed a new email strategy. Results: email open rates increased by 23%, click-through rates by 31%. Strategic initiative

#3: She volunteered to lead a cross-functional project to improve the company's lead generation process. She used AI to research competitor strategies, draft project plans, and create presentations. The project was a success. It generated 40% more qualified leads in the first quarter. Months 7-10: Building Visibility and Getting Promoted (July-October) Jennifer made sure her work was visible. She shared results in team meetings. She documented her strategic initiatives. She asked for feedback from senior leaders. In September, her manager told her they were creating a new role: Marketing Strategist. It was a promotion—more responsibility, more autonomy, and a significant salary increase. They offered it to Jennifer. New title: Marketing Strategist New salary: $72,000 (a 38% increase) New responsibilities: Leading strategic initiatives, managing junior team members, shaping marketing direction She accepted.

The Results: Promotion and 38% Salary Increase in 10 Months

The numbers:

- Before AI: Marketing Coordinator, $52,000/year,

45-50 hours/week, stuck in execution mode

- After AI: Marketing Strategist, $72,000/year,

40-45 hours/week, leading strategic initiatives

- Salary increase: $20,000/year (38%)
- Time to promotion: 10 months

Hours worked: Actually decreased But the real change wasn't just the title or the money. Jennifer told me: "I went from feeling invisible to feeling valued. I went from executing other people's ideas to shaping strategy. I went from wondering if I'd ever advance to being seen as a future leader. That shift in how I'm perceived—that's what really changed my career trajectory."

What Jennifer Learned: The Key Insights

1. "Efficiency creates opportunity." "I didn't set out to get promoted. I just wanted to work smarter. But when I freed up 12 hours per week, I suddenly had time to do the kind of work that gets you noticed. Efficiency wasn't the goal—it was the enabler."

2. "You don't get promoted for working hard. You get promoted for creating impact." "I was working 50-hour weeks before, but I was just keeping up with my current job. When I automated the routine stuff, I could focus on high-impact projects. That's what got me promoted—not the hours I worked, but the value I created."

3. "AI is a competitive advantage if you use it strategically." "Most of my colleagues were still doing everything manually. They were working just as hard as I used to, but they didn't have time for strategic work. I had an unfair advantage because I was using AI to multiply my output. I didn't advertise it—I just used it."

4. "Visibility matters as much as results." "I could have done all that strategic work and stayed invisible. But I made sure my manager and senior leaders knew what I was working on. I shared results. I asked for feedback. I made my impact visible. That's what turned good work into a promotion."

Where Jennifer Is Now

Jennifer has been in her Marketing Strategist role for 14 months. She's now being groomed for a Director-level position. Her salary has increased to $78,000 (after a merit increase). She manages two junior marketers. She's leading the company's entire content and email strategy. She told me: "Two years ago, I was a coordinator wondering if I'd ever advance. Now I'm on track to be a Director by 30. AI didn't get me promoted—my work did. But AI made it possible to do the kind of work that gets you promoted."

Case Study 5: The Creative Who Tripled Output

Meet Sofia: The Burned-Out Designer

Sofia was 29 years old, a freelance graphic designer and illustrator, and she was exhausted. She loved her work. She loved creating. But she was burning out. She was working 50-55 hours per week and earning about $3,800/month. That's roughly $17-19/hour—barely above minimum wage in her city. The problem wasn't that she couldn't find clients. The problem was that she was spending too much time on the wrong things. For every hour of actual creative work—the part she loved—she was spending two hours on everything else: client communication, revisions, administrative tasks, social media, invoicing. And even the creative work was slowing down. She'd hit a creative block. She was recycling the same ideas. She was taking longer to come up with concepts. Sofia told me: "I got into design because I love creating beautiful things. But I was spending most of my time not creating. I was managing clients, doing revisions, posting on Instagram, chasing invoices. The actual design work—the part I loved—was maybe 30% of my time. I was miserable." She considered quitting freelancing and getting a full-time job. At least she'd have a steady pay check and wouldn't have to do all the administrative work herself. But she didn't want to give up the freedom of freelancing. She just wanted to actually enjoy it again. Then she discovered AI tools for creatives.

What Sofia Did: From Burnout to Balance in 5 Months

Month 1: Automating the Administrative Grind (January) Sofia started with the tasks she hated most: client communication and administrative work. Client emails: She used ChatGPT to draft responses to common client requests (project inquiries, revision requests, timeline questions). Time saved: 6 hours/week. Project proposals: She created a template in ChatGPT for project proposals. She'd input project details, and ChatGPT would generate a professional proposal. Time saved: 3 hours/week. Social media captions: She used ChatGPT to write captions for her design posts on Instagram. Time saved: 2 hours/week. Total time saved: 11 hours/week.

Month 2: Using AI to Accelerate Creative Work (February) This is where Sofia was skeptical. She didn't want AI to do her creative work—that was the part she actually enjoyed. But she realized AI could help with the parts of the creative process that were slowing her down: Brainstorming and ideation: When she was stuck on a concept, she'd use ChatGPT to generate ideas. She wouldn't use the AI's ideas directly, but they'd spark her own thinking. Research and inspiration: She'd use ChatGPT to research design trends, colour theory, typography styles. What used to take hours of browsing now took 20 minutes of targeted questions. Mock-ups and variations: She started using AI image generation tools (Midjourney, DALL-E) to quickly create mock-ups and explore visual directions before committing to final designs. She was still doing the creative work. But AI was helping her get unstuck faster and explore more options in less time. Time saved on creative process: 8 hours/week.

Month 3: Reinvesting Time in Higher-Value Work (March) With 19 extra hours per week, Sofia had a choice. She could work less and have more free time. Or she could take on more clients and earn more. She chose a mix: she took on 50% more client work (increasing her income) and used the rest of the time for personal projects and rest. She also raised her rates by 25%. She was delivering work faster and with more creative options, so clients were happy to pay more.

Months 4-5: Scaling and Finding Balance (April-May) Sofia's income increased from $3,800/month to $6,200/month—a 63% increase. But more importantly, she was working 40 hours per week instead of 55. And the work she was doing was more creative, less administrative. She was spending 60% of her time on actual design work (up from 30%). The rest was client communication and business tasks—but those were now streamlined with AI. She told me: "I fell back in love with my work. I'm creating more, earning more, and working less. That's not a trade-off I thought was possible."

The Results: More Income, Less Work, Better Life

The numbers:

- Before AI: $3,800/month, 50-55 hours/week, 30% of time on creative work, burned out After AI: $6,200/month, 40 hours/week, 60% of time on creative work, energized
- Income increase: 63%
- Hours worked: Decreased by 15-20 hours/week
- Creative time: Doubled But the numbers don't capture the full story. Sofia told me: "The money is great, but what really changed is how I feel about my work. I'm not dreading Monday mornings anymore. I'm not working weekends. I have energy for personal projects. I'm creating work I'm actually proud of instead of just churning out client work to pay bills. That's the real win."

What Sofia Learned: The Key Insights

1. "AI doesn't replace creativity. It removes the barriers to creativity." "I was worried AI would make my work feel less authentic or creative. But it didn't. It just removed the friction—the administrative tasks, the creative blocks, the time-consuming research. I'm more creative now because I have more mental energy and time to actually create."

2. "You can scale without sacrificing quality." "I used to think that if I wanted to earn more, I'd have to work more hours or lower my standards. But AI let me scale without either. I'm producing more work in less time, and the quality is actually better because I'm not burned out."

3. "Automation gives you back the parts of your work you love." "I got into design because I love creating. But I was spending most of my time on everything except creating. AI automated the parts I hated, so I could focus on the parts I love. That's not laziness—that's smart."

4. "Balance is possible, but you have to design for it." "I could have used all my extra time to take on more clients and earn even more money. But I chose balance. I chose to work less, create more, and actually enjoy my life. AI made that choice possible."

Where Sofia Is Now

Sofia is now 30. She's earning $7,500-8,000/month, working 35-40 hours per week, and taking on only the projects she's excited about. She's also started teaching other designers how to use AI tools to streamline their workflows. She runs a small online course that generates an additional $1,500/month in passive income. She told me: "A year ago, I was on the verge of quitting freelancing because I was so burned out. Now I can't imagine doing anything else. AI didn't change what I do—it changed how I do it. And that made all the difference."

Patterns Across All Success Stories

You've just read five very different stories:

- A college student who built a freelance business
- A teacher who changed careers
- A solo business owner who scaled
- A corporate employee who got promoted

- A creative who found balance

Different people. Different industries. Different goals. But if you look closely, you'll see patterns. There are common threads running through all these success stories. These patterns are important because they're replicable. They're not about luck or exceptional talent. They're about specific actions and mindsets that anyone can adopt. Let me break down what all these people have in common.

Pattern #1: They Started Before They Felt Ready

Not one of these people waited until they were "experts" in AI. Alex started pitching clients after one month of experimenting with ChatGPT. Priya started building her portfolio before she fully understood content strategy. Marcus began automating his workflow while still figuring out the tools. Jennifer didn't ask for permission to use AI—she just started using it. Sofia was skeptical about AI for creative work, but she tried it anyway. The lesson: You don't need to master AI before you start using it. You learn by doing.

Waiting until you feel "ready" is just another form of procrastination. Start messy. Start imperfect. Start now.

Pattern #2: They Focused on Results, Not Tools

None of these people became obsessed with learning every AI tool that exists. They identified specific problems in their work or life, then found AI tools that could solve those problems. Alex needed to write faster fi ChatGPT for drafting and editing. Priya needed to build new skills quickly fi AI for research and learning acceleration. Marcus needed to free up time fi AI for automating administrative tasks. Jennifer needed to create fi fi strategic impact AI to free up time for high-value work. Sofia needed to reduce burnout AI to automate the parts of work she hated. The lesson: Don't learn AI for the sake of learning AI. Learn it to solve specific problems. Start with your biggest pain point. Find the AI tool that addresses it. Master that one thing. Then move to the next problem.

Pattern #3: They Measured and Tracked Their Progress

Every single person in these case studies tracked their results. Alex tracked his income and client count. Priya documented her portfolio projects and skill development. Marcus did a time audit and measured time savings. Jennifer tracked the impact of her strategic initiatives. Sofia measured her income, hours worked, and percentage of time on creative work. The lesson: What gets measured gets improved. You need to know if what you're doing is working. Track your time savings. Track your income. Track your productivity. Track your results. Without measurement, you're just guessing.

Pattern #4: They Didn't Keep Their AI Use a Secret

Well, some of them did at first. But eventually, they all made their AI competency visible. Alex showcased his AI-enhanced workflow in his portfolio. Priya updated her LinkedIn to highlight her AI skills. Marcus talked about his automation strategies with potential clients. Jennifer made sure her manager knew about the strategic work she was doing (enabled by AI efficiency). Sofia started teaching other designers about AI tools. The lesson: AI competency is valuable, but only if people know you have it. You don't need to announce "I use AI!" in every conversation. But you should make it clear that you're someone who understands modern tools and works efficiently.

Pattern #5: They Reinvested Their Time Savings Strategically

None of these people just used AI to work less and coast. They used the time they saved to create more value: Alex used his extra time to take on more clients and build his business. Priya used her extra time to build skills and a portfolio. Marcus used his extra time to scale his business and hire help. Jennifer used her extra time to work on strategic initiatives that got her promoted. Sofia used her extra time to do more creative work and achieve better balance. The lesson: AI gives you time back. What you do with that time determines your outcome. You can use it to earn more, learn more, create more, or rest more. But use it intentionally.

Pattern #6: They Treated AI as a Tool, Not a Replacement

This is crucial: none of these people let AI do their thinking for them. Alex used AI to draft, but he edited and added his own insights. Priya used AI to accelerate research, but she still read the original sources. Marcus used AI to automate communication, but he maintained personal relationships with clients. Jennifer used AI to free up time, but she did the strategic thinking herself. Sofia used AI to overcome creative blocks, but she made the final creative decisions. The lesson: AI amplifies your capabilities. It doesn't replace your judgment. The value you provide is your thinking, your expertise, your creativity. AI just helps you deliver that value more efficiently.

Pattern #7: They Adjusted and Iterated

None of these people got it right on the first try. Alex's first client pitches were awkward. He refined them. Priya's first portfolio pieces weren't great. She improved them. Marcus's first automation attempts were clunky. He optimized them. Jennifer's first strategic initiatives didn't all succeed. She learned and adjusted. Sofia's first AI-generated ideas weren't usable. She got better at prompting. The lesson: You will make mistakes. That's part of the process. The goal isn't perfection. The goal is progress. Try something. See what works. Adjust. Try again.

Pattern #8: They Had a Bias Toward Action

This is the most important pattern of all. Every single person in these case studies took action quickly. They didn't spend months researching. They didn't wait for the perfect moment. They didn't overthink it. They learned just enough to get started, then they started. The lesson: Action beats analysis. You can read every book about AI. You can watch every tutorial.

You can plan the perfect strategy. But none of that matters if you don't actually do something. The people who win are the ones who start before they're ready, learn as they go, and adjust based on results.

This Is Replicable

Here's what I want you to understand: These stories aren't exceptional. They're examples of what happens when ordinary people use AI tools strategically. Alex isn't a genius. He's a college student who decided to try something new. Priya isn't a tech prodigy. She's a teacher who wanted a career change. Marcus isn't a business savant. He's a freelancer who was tired of being overwhelmed. Jennifer isn't a corporate superstar. She's a young professional who wanted to advance. Sofia isn't a creative genius. She's a designer who was burning out. They're regular people who made a decision: I'm going to learn these tools and use them to create a better life. That's it. That's the whole story. And if they can do it, you can too. You have the same tools they had. You have the same information they had. You have the same opportunities they had. The only question is: will you take action? Because here's the truth: six months from now, you'll either be one of these success stories, or you'll be reading about other people's success stories and wishing you'd started. The choice is yours. In the next chapter, I'm going to give you a concrete 30-day action plan—a step-by-step roadmap to go from where you are now to where these people are. No more theory. No more examples. Just action. Let's finish this.

CHAPTER

08

Your 30-Day AI Action Plan

CHAPTER

This Is Your Starting Line

Let me be direct with you: reading this book won't change your life. I know that sounds harsh, especially after seven chapters of strategies, examples, and inspiration. But it's true. Reading about AI tools won't make you more productive. Reading about prompt engineering won't get you promoted. Reading success stories won't increase your income. Only action will. You can read every book about AI. You can watch every tutorial. You can bookmark every resource. But if you don't actually do something—if you don't open ChatGPT and start experimenting, if you don't automate your first workflow, if you don't build your first project—nothing changes. This chapter is different from everything that came before it. This isn't theory. This isn't inspiration. This isn't "here's what's possible." This is: here's exactly what to do, day by day, for the next 30 days.

Why 30 Days?

Thirty days is long enough to build real skills and see real results. It's short enough that you can commit to it without feeling overwhelmed. In 30 days, you can:

- Set up all the essential AI tools
- Master the fundamentals of prompt engineering
- Automate 2-3 major workflows in your work or school life
- Build a portfolio piece or case study
- Measure tangible time savings and productivity gains
- Develop habits that will serve you for years

But here's what's important: 30 days isn't the finish line. It's the starting line. After 30 days, you won't be an AI expert. You'll be an AI practitioner—someone who knows how to use these tools effectively and has the foundation to keep learning. The goal isn't mastery. The goal is momentum.

How This Plan Works

I've broken the 30 days into four weeks, each with a specific focus:

Week 1: Setup First Wins You'll create accounts, explore interfaces, and complete your first successful AI tasks. The goal is to build confidence and momentum through small, achievable wins.

Week 2: Mastering Prompts Finding Your Use Cases You'll practice prompt engineering across different domains and identify the 3 highest-impact AI applications for your specific situation.

Week 3: Building Workflows Measuring Impact You'll create personalized AI workflows for real tasks, track your time savings, and start building sustainable habits.

Week 4: Scaling Planning Your Next 90 Days You'll work on advanced projects, build portfolio pieces, and create a roadmap for continued growth beyond this plan. Each day has specific tasks that take 30-45 minutes. Some days you might spend more time if you're excited and want to go deeper. Other days you might do the minimum. That's fine. The only rule: do something every day. Even if it's just 15 minutes. Even if you're tired. Even if you don't feel like it. Consistency beats intensity. Small daily actions compound into massive results.

What You'll Need

Before we start, make sure you have: Time commitment:

- 30-45 minutes per day (minimum)
- Ideally at the same time each day to build a habit
- A quiet space where you can focus

Tools:

- A computer or tablet (phone works but isn't ideal)
- Internet connection
- Email address for account signups

- Note-taking app (Notion, Google Docs, or even a physical notebook) Mindset:
- Willingness to experiment and make mistakes
- Commitment to completing all 30 days (even when it gets hard)
- Openness to trying things that feel uncomfortable at first That's it. You don't need money (we'll start with free tools). You don't need technical skills. You just need to show up every day.

A Note on Perfectionism

You're going to want to do this perfectly. You're going to want to understand everything before you try it. You're going to want to wait until you have more time, more knowledge, more confidence. Don't. Done is better than perfect. Action is better than analysis. Your first prompts will be clunky. Your first AI outputs will be mediocre. Your first workflows will be inefficient. That's not just okay—that's expected. That's part of the process. The people in the case studies you just read? They all started messy. They all made mistakes. They all had moments of frustration and confusion. But they kept going. And that's what made the difference. So here's what I want you to commit to: for the next 30 days, prioritize action over perfection. Try things. Break things. Learn from what doesn't work. Adjust. Try again. That's how you actually learn. That's how you actually improve. Ready? Let's begin.

Week 1: Setup & First Wins (Days 1-7)

The goal this week is simple: get your tools set up and experience your first AI-powered wins. You're not trying to master anything. You're just trying to get comfortable with the interfaces, complete a few successful tasks, and build momentum. By the end of this week, you'll have accounts on all the major platforms, you'll have successfully used AI to complete real tasks, and you'll feel confident that you can do this.

Day 1: ChatGPT Setup Your First Conversation

Time required: 30-40 minutes Today's mission: Create your ChatGPT account and have your first successful AI conversation. Step-by-step: 1. Go to chat.openai.com (5 minutes)

- Click "Sign up"
- Use your email or Google account
- Verify your email if needed
- You're in! (Free version is fine for now)

2. Explore the interface (5 minutes)

- Notice the text box at the bottom (that's where you type)
- See the sidebar on the left (that's your conversation history)
- Click "New chat" to start fresh conversations
- That's all you need to know for now

3. Complete your first prompt challenge (20 minutes) Try these three prompts, one at a time. Copy them exactly as written, then read the responses:

Prompt 1 (Warm-up): "Explain what you are and what you can help me with. Keep it simple—I'm brand new to AI." Read the response. Notice how conversational it is.

Prompt 2 (Practical task): "I need to write a professional email to my professor/manager asking for an extension on a project. The project is [describe briefly]. I need 3 more days. Write a polite, professional email that explains the situation without making excuses." Read the response. Notice how it's actually usable. You might need to tweak a few details, but the structure is solid.

Prompt 3 (Creative task): "I'm brainstorming ideas for [a blog post/social media content/a presentation] about [your topic]. Generate 10 creative angles or approaches I could take. Make them specific and interesting." Read the response. Notice how it generates ideas you might not have thought of. 4. Reflect and document (5 minutes) Open a note (digital or physical) and write:

- Which prompt gave you the most useful result?
- What surprised you about ChatGPT's responses?
- What's one task you could use this for tomorrow? Today's win: You've successfully used AI to generate useful content. That's it. That's the milestone. Common issues: fi
- "ChatGPT is slow or not responding" Refresh the page or try again in a few minutes. High traffic can cause delays. fi
- "The response wasn't very good" That's okay! Tomorrow you'll learn to write better prompts. fi
- "I don't know what to ask it" Use the three prompts above. They're designed to work for everyone.

Day 2: Exploring ChatGPT's Range

Time required: 30-40 minutes Today's mission: Discover the breadth of what ChatGPT can do by trying tasks in different categories. Step-by-step: 1. Writing task (10 minutes) Pick one:

- "Write a 200-word introduction for a blog post about [your topic]. Make it engaging and start with a hook that grabs attention."
- "Rewrite this paragraph to be clearer and more concise: [paste your paragraph]"
- "Generate 5 subject lines for an email about [your topic]. Make them attention-grabbing but professional." 2. Research task (10 minutes) Pick one:
- "Summarize the key points of [topic] in bullet points. I need to understand this quickly for [school/work]."
- "What are the main arguments for and against [topic]? Give me both sides in a balanced way."
- "I'm researching [topic]. What are the 5 most important things I should know? Explain each in 2-3 sentences." 3. Problem-solving task (10 minutes) Pick one:
- "I'm trying to [goal], but I'm stuck on [specific problem]. Walk me through 3 different approaches I could try."
- "Help me create a study schedule for the next 2 weeks. I have [list your commitments] and I need to prepare for [exam/project]. Give me a realistic daily breakdown."
- "I need to organize [project/task]. Help me break it down into smaller, manageable steps with a timeline." 4. Reflect and document (5 minutes) Write down:

- Which category (writing, research, problem-solving) was most useful for you?
- What's one specific task from your real life you could use ChatGPT for this week?
- What questions do you still have about how to use this tool? Today's win: You've seen ChatGPT's versatility. You're starting to see where it fits into your actual work or school life.

Day 3: Image Generation with DALL-E

Time required: 30-40 minutes Today's mission: Create your first AI-generated images and understand how image prompts work. Step-by-step:

1. Access DALL-E (5 minutes)

- If you have ChatGPT Plus: DALL-E is built in. Just describe an image in your chat. If you're using free ChatGPT: Go to bing.com/create (Microsoft's free DALL-E access)
- Sign in with your Microsoft account (or create one—it's free)

2. Create your first image (10 minutes) Start simple: "A minimalist logo for a coffee shop called 'Morning Brew' featuring a coffee cup and sunrise, clean lines, modern style" Wait for it to generate (usually 30-60 seconds). Look at the result.

3. Try a more detailed prompt (10 minutes) Now add more specificity: "A professional headshot photo of a young professional in business casual attire, neutral background, natural lighting, confident expression, suitable for LinkedIn profile" Notice how more detail gives you more control over the output.

4. Experiment with style variations (10 minutes) Try the same subject in different styles:

- "[Your subject], photorealistic style"
- "[Your subject], minimalist illustration"
- "[Your subject], watercolour painting style"

See how the style descriptor changes the entire feel.

5. Reflect and document (5 minutes) Write down: What could you use AI image generation for? (Social media graphics? Presentation visuals? Creative projects?)

- What was harder than expected about creating good images? Save your best image somewhere—you'll use it later Today's win: You've created original visual content using AI. Even if it's not perfect, you've proven you can do this. Common issues:
- "My image doesn't look like what I wanted" Try being more specific about style, colors, composition, and mood.
- "I got an error message" fi Some words trigger content filters. Try rephrasing without potentially sensitive terms.

Day 4: Notion AI Setup Organization

Time required: 30-40 minutes Today's mission: Set up Notion and use Notion AI to organize information and generate content. Step-by-step:

1. Create your Notion account (10 minutes) Go to notion.so

- Sign up (free version is fine)
- Choose "For personal use" when asked Skip the templates for now—we'll create our own

2. Create your first AI-powered page (15 minutes)

- Click "+ New page" in the sidebar
- Title it: "AI Learning Journal"
- Type /ai and select "Ask AI to write"
- Try this prompt: "Create a template for tracking my daily AI learning progress, including sections for: what I learned today, what I tried, what worked, what didn't, and tomorrow's goal"
- Notion AI will generate a template. Click "Insert" to add it to your page.

3. Use Notion AI for a real task (10 minutes) Create another new page. Title it with a project or topic you're working on. Try one of these:

- "Help me brainstorm 10 creative angles for [your project/topic]"
- "Summarize the key points I need to cover in [your assignment/presentation]"
- "Create an outline for [your essay/report/article] about [topic]"

4. Reflect and document (5 minutes) In your AI Learning Journal page, fill out today's entry:

- What I learned today: [how Notion AI works]
- What I tried: [the specific prompts you used]
- What worked: [what gave you useful results]
- What didn't: [what needs improvement]
- Tomorrow's goal: [what you'll try next]

Today's win: You've set up an organizational system that uses AI to help you think and plan. This will be your home base for the rest of the 30 days.

Day 5: Grammarly Setup Writing Enhancement

Time required: 30-40 minutes Today's mission: Install Grammarly and see how AI can improve your writing in real-time. Step-by-step: 1. Sign up for Grammarly (10 minutes)

- Go to grammarly.com
- Create a free account
- Install the browser extension (Chrome, Firefox, Safari, or Edge)
- Install the desktop app if you want (optional but useful) 2. Test Grammarly on existing writing (15 minutes) Find something you've written recently—an email, essay draft, social media post, anything. Copy it into a new document at app.grammarly.com
- Watch as Grammarly highlights issues
- Click on each suggestion to see the explanation
- Accept the changes that make sense
- Notice the overall score and how it improves

3. Write something new with Grammarly active (10 minutes) Open your email or a Google Doc (with Grammarly extension active). Write a short professional email or paragraph about anything. Write it quickly without worrying about perfection. Watch as Grammarly:

- Catches typos in real-time
- Suggests better word choices Flags unclear sentences

- Recommends tone adjustments

4. Reflect and document (5 minutes) In your Notion AI Learning Journal:

- What surprised you about Grammarly's suggestions?
- How much time could this save you on a typical writing task?
- What's one thing you write regularly that Grammarly could improve? Today's win: You've added a tool that makes you a better writer automatically. Every email, document, and post you write from now on will be clearer and more professional.

Day 6: Canva AI for Visual Content

Time required: 30-40 minutes Today's mission: Create professional-looking graphics using Canva's AI features. Step-by-step:

1. Sign up for Canva (5 minutes)

- Go to canva.com
- Create a free account
- Skip the pro trial for now (free version has plenty of AI features)

2. Create a social media graphic (15 minutes)

- Click "Create a design" Choose "Instagram Post" (or any social media format)
- Click "Apps" in the left sidebar
- Find "Magic Write" or "Text to Image"
- Try this: "Create a motivational quote graphic about productivity with a modern, minimalist design"

- Canva AI will generate options Customize colors, fonts, or layout if you want
- Download your creation

3. Try the AI background remover (10 minutes)

- Upload any photo (of yourself, an object, anything)
- Click "Edit photo"
- Select "Background Remover" (this is AI-powered)
- Watch as AI automatically removes the background
- Add a new background or leave it transparent Download the result

4. Experiment with Magic Design (5 minutes)

- Start a new design
- Upload an image or choose a topic
- Click "Magic Design" in the toolbar
- Let Canva AI generate multiple design variations
- Browse through the options
- Pick your favourite and customize it

5. Reflect and document (5 minutes) In your journal:

- What could you use Canva AI for regularly? (Social media? Presentations? Thumbnails?)
- How much time did this save compared to designing from scratch?
- Save your best creation—you'll build a portfolio of AI-assisted work Today's win: You've created professional-looking visual content without being a designer. This skill alone can save you hours per week.

Day 7: Week 1 Review First Workflow

Time required: 40-50 minutes Today's mission: Reflect on your first week, identify your biggest win, and create your first simple AI workflow. Step-by-step:

1. Review your week (15 minutes) Open your Notion AI Learning Journal. Read through your entries from Days 1-6. Answer these questions:

- Which tool felt most immediately useful?
- Which task saved you the most time?
- What was harder than you expected?
- What was easier than you expected?
- What are you most excited to explore further?

2. Identify your first workflow (10 minutes) A workflow is just a series of steps you do regularly. Think about your typical week: For students:

- Writing essays (research outline draft edit) Studying for exams (gather materials summarize fi create study guides) fi
- Managing assignments (track deadlines prioritize complete) For professionals
- Email management (read respond follow up)
- Content creation (ideate fi draft fi edit fi publish) fi
- Project planning (define goals break into tasks fi schedule) For freelancers:
- Client communication (inquiries fi proposals fi updates) fi fi fi
- Project delivery (brief create revise deliver)
- Marketing (create content fi post fi engage)

Pick ONE workflow that you do at least once a week. 3. Map your AI-enhanced workflow (15 minutes) Write out the steps of your chosen workflow, then add where AI can help: Example:

Essay writing workflow Old way:

1. Choose topic (30 min)

2. Research (3 hours)

3. Create outline (45 min)

4. Write first draft (4 hours)

5. Edit and revise (1.5 hours)

Total: ~9.5 hours AI-enhanced way:

1. Brainstorm topics with ChatGPT (10 min)

2. Research with ChatGPT summaries + verify sources (1.5 hours)

3. Generate outline with ChatGPT, refine (20 min)

4. Draft with ChatGPT assistance, add personal insights (2 hours)

5. Edit with Grammarly (45 min)

Total: 4.5 hours Now do this for YOUR workflow.

4. Test your workflow (10 minutes) Actually try one step of your new workflow right now. Don't wait. If it's essay writing, brainstorm topics with ChatGPT. If it's email management, draft a response with AI. If it's content creation, generate ideas with Notion AI. Just do one step. Prove to yourself it works.

5. Celebrate your first week (5 minutes) You've completed 7 consecutive days of AI learning. That's not nothing. Write down:

- Your biggest win this week One specific way AI has already saved you time
- What you're committing to for Week 2

Today's win: You've completed

Week 1. You have accounts on all major platforms. You've successfully used AI for real tasks. You've created your first AI-enhanced workflow. You're not a beginner anymore. You're a practitioner.

Week 2: Mastering Prompts Finding Your Use Cases (Days 8-14)

This week is about getting good at the skill that matters most: prompt engineering. You're going to practice writing prompts across different domains. You're going to learn what makes a prompt effective. And you're going to identify the 3 highest-impact AI use cases for your specific situation. By the end of this week, you'll be able to consistently get high-quality outputs from AI tools. You'll know exactly how to ask for what you need.

Day 8: The Anatomy of a Great Prompt

Time required: 30-40 minutes Today's mission: Learn the formula for writing effective prompts and practice applying it. The formula: Great Prompt = Context + Task + Format + Tone + Constraints Let me break that down: Context: What background information does the AI need? Task: What specifically do you want it to do? Format: How should the output be structured? Tone: What style or voice should it use? Constraints: What limitations or requirements? Step-by-step:

1. Study these examples (10 minutes) Bad prompt: "Write about marketing." Good prompt: "I'm a small business owner selling handmade candles. Write a 300-word Instagram caption announcing a new product line of seasonal scents. Use a warm, friendly tone that emphasizes the cozy feeling of fall. Include a call-to-action to visit my website. End with 5 relevant hashtags." See the difference? Bad prompt: "Help me with my essay." Good prompt: "I'm writing a 1500-word argumentative essay for my college English class about the impact of social media on mental health. I need help creating a strong thesis statement that argues social media has a net negative effect on teen mental health. The thesis should be specific, debatable, and set up three main supporting points."

2. Practice the formula (20 minutes) Take these bad prompts and rewrite them using the formula:

Bad prompt 1: "Give me business ideas." Your rewrite: [Context: Who you are, what resources you have] [Task: Generate business ideas] [Format: List with brief descriptions] [Tone: Practical and realistic] [Constraints: Low startup cost, can run part-time] Bad prompt

2: "Write an email." Your rewrite: [Context: Your situation and recipient] [Task: Write a professional email] [Format: Standard business email structure] [Tone: Professional but friendly] [Constraints: Under 150 words, clear call-to-action] Bad prompt

3: "Explain this concept." Your rewrite: [Context: Your current knowledge level] [Task: Explain the concept] [Format: Simple explanation with example] [Tone: Conversational, not academic] [Constraints: Assume no prior knowledge] 3. Test your prompts (10 minutes) Take your rewritten prompts and actually use them in ChatGPT. Compare the results to what you would have gotten with the bad prompts.

4. Document your learning (5 minutes) In your journal:

- Which element of the formula (context, task, format, tone, constraints) made the biggest difference? What's one prompt you use regularly that you can improve using this formula? Today's win: You understand the structure of effective prompts. You can now engineer better results from any AI tool.

Day 9: Prompt Practice - Writing Content

Time required: 30-40 minutes Today's mission: Practice prompt engineering specifically for writing and content creation tasks. Step-by-step:

Challenge 1: Professional email (10 minutes) Write a prompt that generates a professional email for a real situation you're facing (or will face soon). Use the formula: "I'm a [your role] and I need to email [recipient] about [situation]. Write a professional email that [specific goal]. Tone should be [tone]. Keep it under [word count]. Include [specific elements]." Generate the email. Edit it to add personal touches. Save it.

Challenge 2: Social media content (10 minutes) Write a prompt for a social media post about something you're working on or interested in. "Create a [platform] post about [topic] that [goal]. The post should [specific requirements]. Use a [tone] tone. Include [specific elements like hashtags, emoji, call-to-action]." Generate 3 variations. Pick the best one. Customize it.

Challenge 3: Long-form content (10 minutes) Write a prompt for a blog post, article, or essay section. "I'm writing about [topic] for [audience]. Write a 400-word section that [specific purpose]. Start with [hook type]. Include [specific points]. Use [tone]. End with [transition or conclusion]." Generate the content. Notice what works and what needs editing. Reflection (5 minutes) In your journal: Which type of writing prompt was easiest for you?

- What patterns are you noticing in prompts that work well? What's one writing task you do regularly that you

can now do faster with AI? Today's win: You can now generate high-quality written content for any purpose. You're not starting from a blank page anymore.

Day 10: Prompt Practice - Research Analysis

Time required: 30-40 minutes Today's mission: Practice prompts for research, summarization, and analytical tasks. Step-by-step: Challenge 1: Topic overview (10 minutes) Pick a topic you need to understand for school or work. Prompt: "I need to understand [topic] for [purpose]. Give me a comprehensive overview that covers:

1) The basic definition and key concepts,

2) The main perspectives or approaches,

3) Current trends or debates,

4) Practical applications.

Keep each section to 2-3 sentences. Use clear, accessible language." Read the output. Notice how much faster this is than reading multiple articles.

Challenge 2: Comparative analysis (10 minutes) Pick two things you need to compare (products, theories, approaches, etc.). Prompt: "Compare [A] and [B] for someone trying to [goal]. Create a comparison that covers: similarities, key differences, pros and cons of each, and which is better for [specific use case]. Present this as a clear, organized breakdown."

Challenge 3: Summarization (10 minutes) Find a long article, paper, or document you need to read. Prompt: "Summarize this [article/paper/document]: [paste text or provide link]. Focus on:

1) The main argument or thesis,

2) Key supporting points,

3) Important evidence or examples,

4) Conclusions or implications. Keep the summary under 300 words." Reflection (5 minutes) In your journal: How much time did AI save you on research today?

- What's one research task you do regularly that you can now streamline? What did you learn about how to structure research prompts? Today's win: You can now research and analyze information 3-5x faster than before. You're working smarter, not harder.

Day 11: Prompt Practice - Problem-Solving Planning

Time required: 30-40 minutes Today's mission: Practice prompts for strategic thinking, problem-solving, and planning. Step-by-step: Challenge 1: Problem breakdown (10 minutes) Think of a real problem you're facing (school, work, personal project, anything). Prompt: "I'm facing this problem: [describe problem]. Help me break this down by:

1) Identifying the root causes,

2) Listing possible solutions with pros and cons of each,

3) Recommending the best approach and why,

4) Outlining first steps to implement it. Be specific and practical."

Challenge 2: Project planning (10 minutes) Pick a project you need to complete in the next few weeks. Prompt: "I need to [project goal] by [deadline]. I have [resources/constraints]. Create a realistic project plan that includes:

1) Major milestones,

2) Specific tasks broken down by week,

3) Potential obstacles and how to address them,

4) Success metrics. Make it actionable."

Challenge 3: Decision framework (10 minutes) Think of a decision you need to make. Prompt: "I need to decide between [option A] and [option B] for [context]. Help me think through this by:

1) Listing the key factors I should consider,

2) Evaluating each option against those factors,

3) Identifying potential risks or downsides I might be missing,

4) Recommending a decision framework.

Ask me clarifying questions if needed." Reflection (5 minutes) In your journal:

- How did AI help you think more clearly about your problem/project/decision? What's one planning task you do regularly that AI could help with?
- What surprised you about using AI for strategic thinking? Today's win: You can now use AI as a thinking partner for complex problems. You're not just getting answers—you're getting better at asking questions.

Day 12: Prompt Practice – Creative Visual

Time required: 30-40 minutes Today's mission: Practice prompts for creative tasks and visual content generation. Step-by-step:

Challenge 1: Creative brainstorming (10 minutes) Pick a creative project (blog post, video idea, design concept, anything). Prompt: "I'm working on [project] for [audience]. Brainstorm 15 creative angles or approaches I could take. For each idea, include:

1) A catchy title or concept,

2) Why it would resonate with my audience,

3) One unique element that makes it stand out. Be creative and unexpected."

Challenge 2: Visual content prompt (10 minutes) Use DALL-E or Bing Image Creator. Prompt: "Create [type of image] that shows [subject] in [setting]. Style should be [artistic style]. Include [specific elements]. Color palette: [colors]. Mood: [mood/feeling]. Composition: [how elements should be arranged]." Generate 2-3 variations by adjusting different elements.

Challenge 3: Storytelling (10 minutes) Prompt: "Write a compelling 200-word story about [topic/theme] that [emotional goal]. The story should:

1) Start with a relatable situation,

2) Include a moment of tension or challenge,

3) End with a resolution or insight. Use vivid, sensory details. Make it memorable." Reflection (5 minutes) In your journal:

- Which creative prompt gave you the most useful or surprising result?
- How could you use AI to enhance (not replace) your creative process?
- What's one creative task you do regularly that AI could accelerate? Today's win: You can now use AI to overcome creative blocks and generate ideas faster. You're more creative with AI than without it.

Day 13: Identifying Your Top 3 Use Cases

Time required: 40-50 minutes Today's mission: Analyze your past week of practice and identify the 3 highest-impact AI applications for your specific situation. Step-by-step: 1. Review your practice (15 minutes) Look back at Days 8-12. For each day, note:

- Which prompts gave you the most useful results?
- Which tasks saved you the most time?
- Which applications felt most relevant to your actual work/school life? 2. Brainstorm your use cases (15 minutes) Make a list of every task you do regularly (at least once a week) that AI could help with. For students:
- Essay research and outlining
- Study guide creation
- Assignment planning
- Email to professors
- Presentation preparation
- Note summarization
- Exam preparation

For professionals:

- Email management
- Report writing

Meeting preparation

- Project planning
- Client communication

Content creation

- Data analysis

For freelancers:

- Client proposals
- Project briefs
- Content creation
- Social media management

- Administrative tasks
- Marketing copy
- Portfolio updates

3. Prioritize using this framework (10 minutes) For each potential use case, rate it on:

- Frequency: How often do you do this? (1-5)

Time consumption: How long does it take?(1-5)

- AI suitability: How well can AI help? (1-5)
- Impact: How much would time savings matter? (1-5) Add up the scores. Your top 3 scores are your priority use cases.

4. Define your top 3 (10 minutes) For each of your top 3 use cases, write:

Use Case #1: [Name of task]

- Current process: [How you do it now]
- Time it takes: [Hours per week]
- AI-enhanced process: [How AI will help]
- Expected time savings: [Hours per week]
- Tools needed: [Which AI tools]
- First step: [What you'll do tomorrow] Repeat for

Use Cases #2 and #3. 5. Document your plan (5 minutes) In your journal, write: "My top 3 AI use cases are:

1. [Use case] - will save me [X] hours per week

2. [Use case] - will save me [X] hours per week

3. [Use case] - will save me [X] hours per week Total time savings: [X] hours per week" Today's win: You've identified exactly where AI

will have the biggest impact on your life. You're not using AI randomly—you're using it strategically.

Day 14: Week 2 Review Prompt Library

Time required: 40-50 minutes Today's mission: Review your progress, create a personal prompt library, and prepare for Week 3. Step-by-step: 1. Review your week (10 minutes) Answer these questions in your journal:

- How much better are your prompts now compared to Day 8?
- Which type of prompt (writing, research, problem-solving, creative) are you best at?
- What's the most valuable thing you learned about prompt engineering?
- How confident do you feel using AI tools now (1-10)? 2. Create your prompt library (20 minutes) Open a new page in Notion (or a Google Doc) titled "My Prompt Library." Create sections for:
- Writing & Content
- Research & Analysis

Problem-Solving & Planning

- Creative & Visual

Under each section, save your 3-5 best prompts from this week. Format them as templates with [brackets] for the parts you'll customize each time. Example: Writing Content Professional Email Template: "I'm a [your role] and I need to email [recipient] about [situation]. Write a professional email that [specific goal]. Tone should be [tone]. Keep it under [word count]. Include [specific elements]." Do this for all your best prompts. 3. Test your library (10 minutes) Pick one prompt from your library and use it for a real task right now. Prove to yourself that your library works. 4. Set Week 3 goals (10 minutes) Write down:

- My top 3 use cases: [from Day 13]
- This week I'll build workflows for: [pick 2 of your top 3]
- My time-saving goal for Week 3: [specific number of hours]
- One new tool I'll explore: [pick something you haven't tried yet] Today's win: You've completed Week 2. You can now write effective prompts consistently. You have a library of templates you can use anytime. You know exactly where AI will have the biggest impact on your life. You're not just using AI anymore. You're mastering it.

Week 3: Building Workflows &Measuring Impact (Days 15-21)

This week is about turning your AI skills into sustainable systems. You're going to create personalized workflows for your top use cases. You're going to track your time savings. You're going to build habits that will last beyond these 30 days. By the end of this week, AI won't feel like a new tool you're trying out. It'll feel like a natural part of how you work.

Day 15: Building Your First Complete Workflow

Time required: 45-60 minutes Today's mission: Take your #1 use case from Day 13 and build a complete, documented workflow. Step-by-step:

1. Map your current process (10 minutes) Write out every step of how you currently do this task. Example: Writing a blog post Current process:

    1. Stare at blank page trying to think of topic (20 min)
    2. Google research on topic (45 min)
    3. Read 5-7 articles (60 min)
    4. Try to remember what I read (15 min)
    5. Create rough outline (20 min)
    6. Write first draft (90 min)
    7. Edit and revise (30 min)
    8. Proofread (15 min) Total: 4.5 hours

2. Design your AI-enhanced workflow (15 minutes) Rewrite each step with AI assistance. Example: AI-enhanced blog post workflow new process:

    1. n Brainstorm topics with ChatGPT (5 min) Prompt: "Generate 10 blog post ideas about [topic] for [audience]. n Make them specific and actionable."

    2. Research with ChatGPT (15 min) Prompt: "Summarize the key points about [chosen topic]. Include current trends, main perspectives, and interesting angles."

3. Verify key facts with n quick Google search (10 min)

4. Generate outline with ChatGPT (5 min) Prompt: "Create a detailed outline for a blog post about [topic] that [goal]. Include hook, 3-5 main points, and conclusion."

5. Draft with ChatGPT assistance (30 min) n Prompt for each section: "Write [section] that [specific goal]. Use n [tone]. Include [specific elements]." Add personal insights and examples

6. Edit with Grammarly (15 min) 7. Final polish (10 min) Total: 1.5 hours' Time saved: 3 hours per blog post

3. Document your workflow (10 minutes) Create a new page in Notion titled "Workflow: [Your Use Case]" Include:

- Task: [What this workflow is for]
- Frequency: [How often you do this]
- Old time: [How long it used to take]
- New time: [How long it takes with AI]
- Time saved: [Difference]
- Steps: [Your AI-enhanced process with specific

prompts] Tools needed: [List of AI tools]

4. Test your workflow (20 minutes) Actually use your new workflow right now for a real task. Don't wait. Time yourself. Note what works and what needs adjustment.

5. Refine and document (5 minutes) Update your workflow document with:

- What worked well What needs improvement
- Actual time it took

- Any prompts you want to adjust

Today's win: You have a documented, tested workflow that saves you significant time. This isn't theory—it's a system you can use every time you do this task.

Day 16: Building Your Second Workflow

Time required: 45-60 minutes Today's mission: Build a workflow for your #2 use case. Follow the same process as Day 15: 1. Map current process (10 min)

2. Design AI-enhanced workflow (15 min)

3. Document in Notion (10 min)

4. Test with real task (20 min)

5. Refine and document results (5 min) Additional challenge: Look for ways to connect this workflow to your first one. Can you use outputs from one workflow as inputs for another? Example: If Workflow #1 is "Research for essays" and Workflow #2 is "Writing essays," the research output becomes the input for writing. Today's win: You now have two documented workflows. You're building a system, not just using tools randomly.

Day 17: Time Tracking Measurement

Time required: 30-40 minutes Today's mission: Set up a system to track your time savings and measure AI's impact. Step-by-step: 1. Create your tracking sheet (10 minutes) In Notion (or a spreadsheet), create a table with these columns:

- Date
- Task
- Old time (how long it used to take)
- New time (how long it took with AI)
- Time saved
- Tools used
- Notes

2. Log your past workflows (10 minutes) Add entries for the workflows you built on Days 15-16. Include:

- The test runs you did
- Estimated time savings based on your old process
- Any other times you've used AI this week

3. Calculate your current savings (5 minutes) Add up your "Time saved" column. Write down: Total time saved so far: [X hours]

- If I keep this up, I'll save: [X hours per week]
- Over a year, that's: [X hours per year]

4. Set measurement goals (10 minutes) Write down:

- By Day 21, I want to save: [X hours per week]
- By Day 30, I want to save: [X hours per week]
- The task I most want to speed up: [specific task]
- How I'll use my saved time: [specific plan]

5. Commit to daily tracking (5 minutes) For the rest of the 30 days, spend 2-3 minutes at the end of each day logging any AI-assisted tasks in your tracking sheet. This takes almost no time, but it keeps you motivated by showing your progress. Today's win: You're now

measuring your results. What gets measured gets improved. You'll be amazed how motivating it is to see your time savings add up.

Day 18: Habit Building Integration

Time required: 30-40 minutes Today's mission: Integrate AI into your daily routine so it becomes automatic, not something you have to remember to do. Step-by-step:

1. Identify your trigger moments (10 minutes) Think about your typical day. When do you do the tasks that AI can help with? Examples:

- "Every morning when I check email" Use ChatGPT for responses
- "Every time I start writing" Open Grammarly

"Every time I need to research something" Start with ChatGPT summary

- "Every time I plan my week" Use Notion AI for organization Write down 5 trigger moments in your day when you should use AI.

2. Create implementation intentions (10 minutes) For each trigger, write an "if-then" statement: Format: "If [trigger situation], then I will [specific AI action]." Examples:

- "If I need to write a professional email, then I will draft it in ChatGPT first."
- "If I'm starting a research task, then I will ask ChatGPT for an overview before Googling."
- "If I'm planning my day, then I will use Notion AI to organize my tasks." Write 5 implementation intentions.

3. Set up environmental cues (10 minutes) Make it easier to remember to use AI:

- Pin ChatGPT tab in your browser
- Add Notion to your bookmarks bar Set Grammarly to auto-start
- Create a desktop shortcut to your prompt library
- Add a daily reminder on your phone: "Did you

use AI today?"

4. Practice your new habits (10 minutes) Right now, go through your trigger moments and practice the AI action for each one. Don't wait for the trigger to happen naturally—simulate it. Today's win: You've designed your environment and routines to make AI usage automatic. You're building habits that will last long after these 30 days.

Day 19: Troubleshooting Optimization

Time required: 30-40 minutes Today's mission: Identify what's not working in your workflows and fix it. Step-by-step:

1. Review your workflows (10 minutes) Look at the workflows you built on Days 15-16. Answer honestly:

- Which steps are still clunky or slow?
- Where are you still getting mediocre AI outputs?
- What parts of the workflow do you skip or avoid?
- What's taking longer than expected?

2. Diagnose the problems (10 minutes) For each issue, identify the root cause: Common problems: Vague prompts Need more specificity

- Wrong tool for the task Try a different AI

tool

- Too many steps Simplify the workflow
- Outputs need too much editing fi Improve

your prompts

- Forgetting to use the workflow Need better

triggers/reminders 3. Fix one problem (15 minutes) Pick your biggest workflow problem and fix it right now. If it's vague prompts:

- Rewrite your prompts using the formula from

Day 8 Test the new prompts

- Update your workflow document

If it's the wrong tool:

- Research alternative AI tools for that task
- Try one alternative
- Compare results

If it's too many steps: Look for steps you can combine or eliminate

- Test the simplified workflow
- Update your documentation

4. Document your improvements (5 minutes) In your journal:

- What problem did you fix today?
- What was the solution?
- How much better is the workflow now?

Today's win: You're not just using AI—you're optimizing your systems. This is how you go from good results to great results.

Day 20: Expanding Your Toolkit

Time required: 30-40 minutes Today's mission: Explore one new AI tool or feature you haven't tried yet. Options to explore: Option 1: Advanced ChatGPT features

- Custom instructions (tell ChatGPT how to always respond to you)
- Code interpreter (for data analysis)
- Plugins (if you have ChatGPT Plus)

Option 2: Specialized AI tools

- Perplexity AI (AI-powered search with sources) Claude (alternative to ChatGPT with different strengths)
- Jasper or Copy.ai (specialized for marketing copy)

Option 3: AI browser extensions Compose AI (write emails faster)

- Merlin (ChatGPT in your browser sidebar)
- Wiseone (AI reading assistant)

Option 4: Industry-specific AI

- GitHub Copilot (for coding)
- Descript (for video/audio editing)
- Runway ML (for video generation)

Step-by-step: 1. Choose one tool (5 minutes) Pick based on:

- What would be most useful for your work/school? What sounds most interesting?
- What could fill a gap in your current toolkit?

2. Set it up (10 minutes)

- Create account if needed

- Install extension/app if applicable
- Complete any onboarding or tutorial

3. Complete a test task (15 minutes) Use the new tool for a real task. Don't just explore—actually create something. 4. Evaluate and document (10 minutes) In your journal:

- What tool did you try?
- What did you use it for?
- How does it compare to tools you're already using?
- Will you add this to your regular toolkit? Why or why not? Today's win: You're expanding your capabilities. You're not limited to the tools you started with—you're continuously exploring and adapting.

Day 21: Week 3 Review Reflection

Time required: 40-50 minutes Today's mission: Reflect on your progress, celebrate your wins, and prepare for the final week. Step-by-step:

1. Review your time savings (10 minutes) Open your tracking sheet from Day 17. Calculate: Total time saved this week

- Total time saved since Day 1
- Average time saved per day Projected annual time savings

Write these numbers down. Look at them. Let them sink in.

2. Reflect on your transformation (15 minutes) Answer these questions in your journal: About skills:

- How confident do you feel using AI now (1-10)?

What's the biggest skill you've developed?

- What can you do now that you couldn't do 3

weeks ago? About workflows:

- Which workflow has had the biggest impact?
- What's working better than expected?
- What still needs improvement?

About habits: Is AI becoming automatic for you?

- What triggers are working well?
- What habits still need reinforcement?

3. Identify your biggest win (10 minutes) Think about the past 3 weeks. What's the single biggest win? Maybe it's:

- A specific project you completed faster
- A skill you developed

Time you saved

- Confidence you gained
- A problem you solved

Write about it in detail. What happened? How did AI help? How do you feel about it?

4. Set Week 4 goals (10 minutes) Write down:

- One workflow I'll perfect this week: [specific workflow]
- One advanced skill I'll develop: [specific skill]
- One portfolio piece I'll create: [specific project]
- My time-saving goal for Week 4: [specific number]

5. Celebrate (5 minutes) You've completed 21 consecutive days of AI learning and practice. That's not easy. Most people quit long before this point. Write down: "I'm proud of myself for [specific

accomplishment]. Three weeks ago, I couldn't [specific skill]. Now I can [specific capability]. That's real progress." Today's win: You've completed Week 3. You have working workflows. You're measuring your impact. AI is becoming a habit. You're not just learning anymore—you're performing. One more week. Let's finish strong.

Week 4: Scaling Planning Your Next 90 Days (Days 22-28)

This is your final week of the 30-day plan. But it's not an ending—it's a launching pad. This week, you're going to work on advanced projects, create portfolio pieces that demonstrate your AI competency, and build a roadmap for continued growth. By Day 30, you'll have concrete proof of your AI skills and a clear plan for the next 90 days.

Day 22: Advanced Project - Part 1

Time required: 60-90 minutes Today's mission: Start a project that combines multiple AI tools and showcases your skills. Project options: For students:

- Create a comprehensive study guide for your hardest class using ChatGPT, Notion AI, and Canva
- Write and design a research paper with AI assistance, documenting your process
- Build a personal website showcasing your work using AI tools for professionals:

- Create a complete content marketing campaign (blog post, social media, graphics) using AI
- Develop a process improvement proposal for your team showing AI automation opportunities
- Build a portfolio of AI-enhanced work samples

For freelancers:

- Create a client onboarding system using AI tools
- Develop a content creation workflow that you can sell as a service Build a case study showing before/after of your AI-enhanced process Step-by-step: 1. Choose your project (10 minutes) Pick something that:
- Demonstrates multiple AI skills

Solves a real problem

- You can complete in 3-4 days
- You'd be proud to show others

2. Plan your project (20 minutes) Create a project plan:

- Goal: What you're creating
- Why: What problem it solves
- Tools: Which AI tools you'll use
- Timeline: What you'll do each day (Days 22-25)
- Success criteria: How you'll know it's done

3. Start building (30-60 minutes) Begin working on your project. Focus on the first major component. Use your workflows. Use your prompt library. Apply everything you've learned. 4. Document your process (10 minutes) As you work, take notes on:

- Which AI tools you're using

- What prompts are working well Time you're saving
- Challenges you're encountering

This documentation will be valuable later. Today's win: You've started an advanced project that will showcase your AI skills. This is portfolio-worthy work.

Day 23: Advanced Project - Part 2

Time required: 60-90 minutes Today's mission: Continue building your project, focusing on quality and polish. Step-by-step: 1. Review yesterday's work (10 minutes) Look at what you created on Day 22. What's working? What needs improvement? 2. Continue building (50-70 minutes) Work on the next major component of your project. Tips for quality:

- Don't just accept first AI outputs—iterate and refine
- Add your personal insights and expertise Make sure everything aligns with your goal
- Focus on creating something you'd actually use or show to others 3. Get feedback (10 minutes) If possible, show your work-in-progress to someone (friend, colleague, classmate). Ask: Does this make sense?
- What's working well?
- What could be better?

4. Document progress (10 minutes) Update your project notes:

- What you completed today
- What's left to do
- Any new insights about using AI
- Estimated time saved so far

Today's win: Your project is taking shape. You're creating something substantial that demonstrates your AI competency.

Day 24: Advanced Project - Part 3

Time required: 60-90 minutes Today's mission: Complete your project and prepare it for presentation. Step-by-step: 1. Finish building (40-60 minutes) Complete any remaining components of your project. Focus on:

- Completeness (did you achieve your goal?) Quality (is this something you're proud of?)
- Polish (does it look professional?)

2. Create a "making of" document (20-30 minutes) This is important. Create a document that explains: Project Overview: What you created

- What problem it solves
- Who it's for

AI Tools Used:

- List of tools
- How you used each one

Why you chose them

Process:

- Your workflow
- Key prompts you used
- Challenges and solutions

Results:

- Time saved compared to doing it manually

Quality improvements

- What you learned

3. Save everything (10 minutes) Organize your project files: Final deliverable

- "Making of" document
- Screenshots of your process

Any prompts or templates you created Save it all in a folder you can easily find later. Today's win: You've completed an advanced project that showcases your AI skills. This is proof of your competency.

Day 25: Building Your AI Portfolio

Time required: 45-60 minutes Today's mission: Create a portfolio that showcases your AI work and competency. Step-by-step:

1. Gather your best work (15 minutes) Collect examples from the past 25 days:

- Your advanced project from Days 22-24
- Your best workflows

Before/after examples showing AI improvements

- Time-saving metrics
- Any other impressive results

2. Choose your platform (10 minutes)

Options:

- Notion page (easiest, free, looks professional) Google Site (free, simple)

- Personal website (more advanced, but impressive)
- LinkedIn featured section (great for job seekers) Pick one and set it up.

3. Create your portfolio (25-35 minutes) Structure: Introduction:

- Brief bio
- Why you're learning AI

What you can do with AI tools

Skills:

- AI tools you're proficient in
- Types of tasks you can handle
- Your specialties

Projects:

- Your advanced project (with "making of" document)
- 2-3 other strong examples
- For each: what you created, tools used, results achieved Metrics: Total time saved
- Productivity improvements
- Any other quantifiable results

Contact:

- How people can reach you
- What you're available for (if freelancing)

4. Polish and publish (10 minutes) Proofread everything

- Make sure links work
- Add any images or screenshots Publish or share

Today's win: You have a portfolio that demonstrates your AI competency. This is something you can show to employers, clients, or anyone who asks "what can you do with AI?"

Day 26: LinkedIn Optimization

Time required: 45-60 minutes Today's mission: Update your LinkedIn profile to showcase your AI skills and attract opportunities. Step-by-step:

1. Update your headline (10 minutes) Before: "Marketing Coordinator at XYZ Company" After: "Marketing Coordinator | AI-Enhanced Content Strategy | Helping brands scale content production with AI tools" Make it clear you have AI skills.

2. Rewrite your About section (15 minutes) Add a paragraph about your AI competency: Example: "Over the past month, I've developed expertise in AI-powered workflows, specializing in [your focus area]. I use tools like ChatGPT, Notion AI, and Canva AI to [specific benefits you deliver]. This approach has allowed me to [specific results: increase output by X%, reduce time by X hours, etc.]. I'm passionate about leveraging AI to work smarter and deliver better results."

3. Add AI skills (10 minutes) In the Skills section, add:

- ChatGPT
- Prompt Engineering
- AI-Assisted Content Creation
- Notion AI
- AI Workflow Automation
- [Any other relevant AI tools]

Ask 2-3 connections to endorse these skills.

4. Update your Experience section (15 minutes) For your current/recent roles, add bullet points about AI: Examples:

- "Implemented AI-assisted content workflow,

increasing output by 150% while maintaining quality"

- "Developed prompt engineering framework for

consistent brand voice across AI-generated content"

- "Reduced research time by 60% using

AI-powered summarization and analysis tools"

5. Add your portfolio (10 minutes) In the Featured section, add:

- Link to your AI portfolio
- Your advanced project
- Any impressive AI-assisted work

Today's win: Your LinkedIn profile now signals that you're ahead of the curve on AI. Recruiters and opportunities will start finding you.

Day 27: Planning Your Next 90 Days

Time required: 45-60 minutes Today's mission: Create a roadmap for continued AI learning and application beyond these 30 days. Step-by-step:

1. Reflect on your progress (15 minutes) Answer these questions: Skills:

- What AI skills have you developed?

What are you best at?

- What do you still want to learn?

Impact:

- How much time are you saving per week?
- What's the biggest way AI has helped you?
- What opportunities has AI created?

Habits: Which AI habits have stuck?

- What's still inconsistent?
- What needs reinforcement?

2. Set 90-day goals (15 minutes) Write down specific, measurable goals for the next 3 months: Skill goals:

- "Master advanced prompt engineering

techniques"

- "Learn [specific AI tool] for [specific purpose]"

"Develop expertise in [specific application]"

Impact goals:

- "Save 10+ hours per week through AI

automation" "Complete [specific project] using AI"

- "Increase [specific metric] by X% using AI"

Career goals:

- "Get promoted by demonstrating AI-enhanced

productivity"

- "Land [number] freelance clients by showcasing

AI skills" "Transition to [specific role] that leverages AI"

3. Create your learning curriculum (15 minutes) Plan what you'll learn each month: Month 1 (Days 31-60):

- Focus: [specific skill or tool]
- Projects: [what you'll build]
- Goal: [specific outcome]

Month 2 (Days 61-90):

- Focus: [next skill or tool]

Projects: [what you'll build]

- Goal: [specific outcome]

Month 3 (Days 91-120):

- Focus: [advanced skill or specialization]
- Projects: [what you'll build]
- Goal: [specific outcome]

4. Identify resources (10 minutes) List resources you'll use: Online courses or tutorials

- AI communities or forums
- Books or blogs

People you can learn from

5. Schedule your learning (10 minutes) Block time in your calendar:

- Daily AI practice (15-30 minutes)
- Weekly project time (2-3 hours)
- Monthly review and planning (1 hour)

Make it non-negotiable. Today's win: You have a clear roadmap for the next 90 days. You're not stopping at 30 days—you're just getting started.

Day 28: Week 4 Review Final Preparations

Time required: 45-60 minutes Today's mission: Review your final week, prepare for Day 30, and set yourself up for long-term success. Step-by-step:

1. Review Week 4 (15 minutes) Look back at Days 22-27. Answer:

- What did you accomplish this week?
- What are you most proud of?
- What was harder than expected?
- What surprised you?

2. Calculate your total impact (15 minutes) Open your time tracking sheet. Calculate: Total time saved over 30 days: [X hours]

- Average time saved per week: [X hours]
- Projected annual time savings: [X hours]

Monetary value (time saved × your hourly rate):

[$X] Write these numbers down. This is your ROI from 30 days of AI learning. 3. Identify your biggest transformation (10 minutes) Think about who you were on Day 1 vs. who you are now. Write: "30 days ago, I [what you couldn't do]. Now I [what you can do]. The biggest change is [specific transformation]." 4. Prepare for Day 30 (10 minutes) Day 30 will be your final reflection and commitment. To prepare: Review your 90-day plan

- Think about what you want to commit to
- Consider what success looks like for you

5. Celebrate your progress (10 minutes) You've completed 28 days. You've built skills, created workflows, saved time, and demonstrated competency. Write down:

- 3 specific accomplishments you're proud of
- 3 ways AI has already improved your life 3 opportunities AI has created for you

Today's win: You're ready for Day 30. You've done the work. You've seen the results. You're prepared to commit to long-term success.

Day 29: Buffer Day Catch-Up

Time required: Flexible Today's mission: Use today to catch up on anything you missed or want to revisit. Options: If you're behind:

- Complete any days you skipped
- Finish your advanced project

Update your portfolio or LinkedIn

If you're on track:

- Revisit a workflow that needs improvement
- Explore a new AI tool
- Practice advanced prompting techniques
- Help someone else get started with AI

If you're ahead:

- Start working on your 90-day goals

Build an additional portfolio piece

- Write about your AI learning journey
- Plan how you'll teach others what you've learned

Today's win: You're using this buffer day intentionally. You're not coasting—you're optimizing.

Day 30: Final Reflection Commitment

Time required: 60-90 minutes Today's mission: Reflect on your 30-day journey and commit to your next steps. Step-by-step: 1. Complete your final reflection (30 minutes) Answer these questions in detail: About the journey: What was the most valuable thing you learned?

- What was the biggest challenge you overcame?
- What surprised you most about AI?

What would you tell someone starting this journey? About your transformation:

- How have you changed in 30 days?

What can you do now that you couldn't do before?

- How has AI impacted your work/school/life?
- What opportunities have opened up?

About the future:

- What are you most excited about?
- What do you want to master next?

How will you continue learning?

- What's your vision for where AI can take you?

2. Review your metrics (15 minutes) Look at all your numbers:

- Time saved
- Workflows created
- Projects completed
- Skills

developed Tools mastered

- Portfolio pieces created

Write them all down in one place. Look at them. Really see what you've accomplished. Calculate your total impact: Total hours saved: [Add up all your time savings]

- Weekly time savings: [Divide by 4 to get average per week] Projected annual savings: [Multiply weekly savings by 52]
- Monetary value: [Hours saved × your hourly rate] Example: Total hours saved: 47 hours
- Weekly average: ~12 hours
- Annual projection: 624 hours (that's 15.6 full work weeks)
- Monetary value: 624 hours × $25/hour = $15,600 These aren't just numbers.

This is your life. This is time you get back to spend on what matters—advancing your career, building skills, spending time with people you love, pursuing passions, or simply resting.

3. Create your commitment statement (15 minutes) This is important. You're going to write a commitment to yourself about what comes next. Use this template or create your own: My AI Commitment Statement Date: [Today's date] What I've accomplished in 30 days: [List 3-5 specific achievements] What AI has made possible for me: [Describe the impact—time saved, opportunities created, confidence gained] My commitment for the next 90 days: I commit to:

1. [Specific skill I'll develop]

2. [Specific workflow I'll perfect]

3. [Specific goal I'll achieve using AI] How I'll measure success: [Specific metrics—time saved, projects completed, income increased, etc.] What I'll do when I face obstacles: [Your plan for

staying consistent when motivation dips] My vision for one year from now: [Where you see yourself, what you'll be capable of,

how AI will be integrated into your life] Signed: [Your name] Write this out. Sign it. Take a photo of it. Put it somewhere you'll see it. This isn't just a document. It's a promise to yourself. 4. Celebrate your wins (10 minutes) You've completed 30 consecutive days of learning and implementation. That's not nothing. Most people don't finish what they start. But you did. Take a moment to acknowledge what that means:

- You showed up every day, even when it was hard
- You learned new skills that most people are still afraid to touch
- You built workflows that are saving you real time
- You created work you're proud of

You positioned yourself ahead of 95% of your peers Write down your three biggest wins from these 30 days. Not what you think you should say—what actually matters to you. My three biggest wins:

1. [Your first win]

2. [Your second win]

3. [Your third win] Now celebrate. Seriously. Do something to mark this achievement:

- Share your progress with someone who supported you
- Treat yourself to something you've been wanting
- Take a day off to rest and recharge Post about your journey on social media
- Just sit with the satisfaction of knowing you did this You earned this moment.

5. Plan your first week after Day 30 (15 minutes) The 30-day plan ends, but your AI journey doesn't. Here's how to maintain momentum:

Days 31-37: Consolidation Week

Day 31: Review all your workflows. Which ones are working perfectly? Which need refinement?

Day 32: Update your prompt library with any new prompts you've discovered. Organize them by category.

Day 33: Reach out to someone in your network. Share what you've learned. Offer to help them get started with AI.

Day 34: Start your first 90-day goal. Take the first concrete action toward the skill or project you committed to.

Day 35: Explore one new AI tool or feature you haven't tried yet. Stay curious.

Day 36: Review your time tracking. Are you maintaining your time savings? If not, why? Adjust your workflows.

Day 37: Weekly reflection. What worked this week? What needs adjustment? What's your focus for next week? Write this plan in your calendar right now. Block the time. Make it non-negotiable.

6. Document your journey (10 minutes) Before you close this chapter, document your 30-day journey in a way you can look back on: Create a "30-Day Transformation" document that includes:

- Your starting point (Day 1 reflections)
- Your biggest challenges and how you overcame them
- Your favorite prompts and workflows

- Screenshots or examples of your best work

Your metrics and time savings

- Lessons learned
- Advice for your future self

Save this somewhere safe. You'll want to look back on it in 6 months, a year, five years. You'll be amazed at how far you've come. Today's win: You've completed the 30-day plan. You're not the same person who started this journey. You have new skills, new confidence, new possibilities. But here's what matters most: You've proven to yourself that you can do this. You can learn. You can adapt. You can thrive in a world that's changing faster than ever. The 30 days are over. Your AI-powered future is just beginning.

Trouble shooting: Common Problems Solutions

You're going to run into problems. Everyone does. Here are the most common issues people face when learning AI, and exactly how to solve them.

Problem 1: "The AI isn't giving me good results"

Why this happens: Your prompts are probably too vague, or you're not giving the AI enough context to understand what you actually need. The solution: Go back to the prompt engineering fundamentals from Chapter 4. Every prompt needs: 1. Context: Who you are, what you're working on, what the situation is 2. Task: Exactly what you want the AI to do 3. Format: How you want the output structured 4. Tone: What style or voice you need 5. Constraints: Any limitations or requirements Try this right now: Take your last disappointing AI output. Rewrite your prompt using all five elements above. Compare the results. Example transformation: Vague prompt: "Write a blog post about productivity." Better prompt: "I'm a freelance writer creating content for small business owners who struggle with time management. Write a 500-word blog post about using AI tools to automate repetitive tasks. Use a conversational, encouraging tone.

Include 3 specific examples of tasks that can be automated. End with a clear call-to-action encouraging readers to try one automation this week." See the difference? The second prompt gives the AI everything it needs to create something useful. If you're still getting poor results: Try a different AI tool (ChatGPT vs. Claude vs.

Bard—they have different strengths)

- Break your request into smaller steps
- Provide examples of what you want
- Ask the AI to ask you clarifying questions before generating

Problem 2: "I'm overwhelmed by too many tools and options"

Why this happens: You're trying to learn everything at once instead of mastering the essentials first. The solution: Simplify. Radically. For the next 30 days, use ONLY these three tools:

1. ChatGPT (for writing, research, problem-solving)

2. Notion AI (for organization and note-taking)

3. Grammarly (for polishing your writing) That's it.

Three tools. Master them completely before adding anything else. Here's your simplified workflow:

- All writing and brainstorming ChatGPT
- All organization and documentation Notion AI
- All editing and proofreading Grammarly

Once these three feel natural and automatic, then—and only then—add one new tool. Remember: It's better to be excellent with three tools than mediocre with fifteen.

Problem 3: "I started strong but my motivation is fading"

Why this happens: You're not seeing results fast enough, or you're not tracking your progress, or the novelty has worn off. The solution: Reconnect with your "why" and make your progress visible. Do this today:

1. Write down why you started: What problem were you trying to solve? What opportunity were you chasing? What were you afraid of missing out on?

2. Calculate your actual time savings: Go back through your tracking sheet. Add up every minute AI has saved you. Convert it to hours. Look at that number.

3. Identify one concrete win: What's one thing you can do now that you couldn't do 30 days ago? Write it down. Be specific.

4. Set a micro-goal for tomorrow: Not "Master AI"—something tiny like "use ChatGPT to draft one email" or "create one social media graphic with Canva AI." Create a motivation trigger: Every morning,

before you check email or social media, open your AI tool of choice and complete one small task. Just one. Build the habit of starting your day with an AI win. Join a community: Find other people learning AI. Share your progress. Celebrate wins together. Accountability makes everything easier.

- AI learning communities on Discord or Reddit
- LinkedIn groups focused on AI skills

Local meetups or study groups

- Even just one friend who's also learning

You're not alone in this. Connect with others on the same journey.

Problem 4: "I feel like an imposter—everyone else seems so much better at this"

Why this happens: You're comparing your beginning to someone else's middle. You're seeing their polished outputs without seeing the messy process behind them. The solution: Reframe what "good at AI" actually means. Here's the truth: Nobody is "naturally good" at AI. It's a skill you build through practice. Every expert you see was once exactly where you are now—confused, uncertain, making mistakes. The difference between you and them: They kept going. That's it. Do this exercise: Look back at your Day 1 work. Compare it to your Day 30 work. See the improvement? That's real growth. That's proof you're getting better. Remember:

- You don't need to be the best. You just need to be better than you were yesterday. Your "beginner" work is better than the work of someone who never started.
- Imposter syndrome means you care about

quality. That's a good thing. Practical tip: Stop consuming and start creating. Every hour you spend watching AI tutorials or reading about AI is an hour you're not actually using AI. Close the tabs. Open ChatGPT. Make something. Anything. Action cures imposter syndrome.

Problem 5: "I'm not seeing the time savings everyone talks about"

Why this happens: You're either not tracking accurately, not using AI for the right tasks, or still doing things the old way out of habit. The solution: Audit your workflow and track everything for one week. Do this: For the next 7 days, track every task you do. Write down: What the task was

- How long it took
- Whether you used AI If not, why not

At the end of the week, review your list. You'll probably find: 1. Tasks you're still doing manually that AI could handle: These are your opportunities. Pick the top 3 and create AI workflows for them this week. 2. Tasks where you're using AI inefficiently: Maybe you're editing AI outputs too much, or your prompts aren't specific enough. Refine your approach. 3. Tasks where AI genuinely isn't helpful: That's fine. Not everything should be automated. Focus your AI efforts on the tasks where it actually saves time. The real question isn't "Is AI saving me time?" It's "Am I using AI for the right things?" Quick wins to try this week:

- Use ChatGPT to draft all your emails (save 20-30 min/day)
- Use Notion AI to organize your notes and tasks (save 15-20 min/day)

- Use Grammarly to edit everything you write (save 10-15 min/day) That's 45-65 minutes per day. Over a week, that's 5-7 hours. Over a year, that's 260-390 hours. The time savings are real. You just have to actually use the tools.

Problem 6: "AI keeps making mistakes or giving me wrong information"

Why this happens: AI tools are powerful, but they're not perfect. They can generate plausible-sounding information that's actually incorrect. The solution: Never trust AI blindly. Always verify, especially for facts, data, or anything important. Your verification checklist:

- For facts and data: Cross-reference with reliable sources. Use AI to draft, but verify the details yourself. For creative work: Use AI to generate ideas and first drafts, but apply your own judgment and expertise.
- For code: Test everything. AI-generated code often works but sometimes has subtle bugs.
- For professional communication: Read everything before sending. Make sure it sounds like you and says what you actually mean. Think of AI as a very smart intern:
- Great at research and first drafts
- Needs supervision and fact-checking
- Sometimes confidently wrong
- Improves with clear instructions

You're the expert. AI is the assistant. Never forget that relationship.

Problem 7: "I don't have time to learn all this"

Why this happens: You're thinking of AI as something extra you have to do, instead of something that saves you time on what you're already doing. The solution: You don't need extra time. You need to replace old methods with AI-enhanced methods. Instead of adding AI to your schedule, integrate it:

- Don't: "I'll spend 30 minutes learning AI, then do my work"
- Do: "I'll use AI while doing my work and learn as I go" Start with one task you do every day:

- If you write emails daily fi Use ChatGPT to draft them
- If you create content Use AI to generate ideas and outlines
- If you do research fi Use AI to summarize and

organize information Time investment:

- Week 1: Might take slightly longer as you learn

Week 2: Breaking even with your old method

- Week 3+: Saving significant time

The time you "spend" learning AI is actually time you're investing in saving exponentially more time later. You don't have time NOT to learn this.

You're Not Just Reading—You're Becoming

Let me tell you what just happened. You didn't just read a book about AI. You didn't just learn some tools or memorize some prompts. You transformed. Think about where you were when you started this book. Maybe you were:

- Anxious about AI replacing your job
- Overwhelmed by how fast technology is changing
- Watching others succeed with AI while you felt left behind
- Uncertain about where to even start Skeptical that you could actually learn this

And now? Now you have AI tools set up and ready to use. You have workflows that save you hours every week. You have prompts that generate professional-quality work. You have a portfolio that demonstrates your capabilities. You have a plan for the next 90 days. But more than that—you have proof. Proof that you can learn new skills. Proof that you can adapt to change. Proof that you can thrive in uncertainty. That's what this was really about.

The Journey You Just Completed

Let's look back at what you've accomplished: Chapter 1: You confronted the reality that AI is reshaping the world of work. You made the decision to adapt instead of resist. Chapter 2: You destroyed the myths that were holding you back. You realized AI isn't replacing humans—it's amplifying the humans who know how to use it. Chapter 3: You learned about the essential tools and set them up. You went from "I don't know where to start" to "I have a working AI toolkit." Chapter 4: You mastered prompt engineering—the skill that separates people who get mediocre results from people who get exceptional results. Chapter 5: You built automation workflows that save you real time on real tasks. You learned to work smarter, not harder. Chapter 6: You positioned yourself for the future. You learned about emerging roles, developed future-proof skills, and built a personal brand that signals your AI competency. Chapter 7: You saw yourself in the success stories. You realized that ordinary people are doing extraordinary things with AI—and you can too. Chapter 8: You took action. For 30 days, you showed up. You practiced. You built. You measured. You proved to yourself that you can do this. That's not just reading. That's transformation.

What Makes You Different Now

You're not the same person who started this book. Here's what's changed: You have skills that most people don't have. While others are still afraid of AI or dismissing it as a fad, you're fluent in the tools that are reshaping every industry. You have confidence that comes from doing. You didn't just learn theory—you built real workflows, created real projects, saved real time. You have proof of your capabilities. You have a competitive advantage. In job applications, freelance pitches, salary negotiations, project bids—you can do things faster and better than people who haven't learned these skills. You have momentum. You've built habits that will serve you for years. You've proven you can learn and adapt. That momentum compounds. You have a future-proof mindset. You're not afraid of change anymore. You know that when new tools emerge, you can learn them. When industries shift, you can adapt. That's what this book gave you. Not just AI skills—but the confidence and capability to thrive in a world that never stops changing.

This Is Just the Beginning

Here's what I need you to understand: The 30-day plan isn't the end of your AI journey. It's the beginning. You've built the foundation. Now you get to build whatever you want on top of it. In the next 90 days, you could: Master advanced AI techniques that put you in the top 5% of users

- Build a portfolio of AI-enhanced work that lands you better opportunities Automate so much of your workflow that you reclaim 10+ hours per week
- Develop expertise in AI applications for your specific industry Start teaching others and position yourself as an expert in the next year, you could:
- Transition into a higher-paying role that values your AI skills Launch a side business built on AI-enhanced productivity
- Become the go-to person in your organization for AI implementation Save hundreds of hours and redirect that time toward what matters most
- Build a career that's not just secure—it's thriving In the next five years, you could:
- Be leading teams that leverage AI to solve complex problems
- Be earning significantly more because of your AI expertise
- Be creating opportunities that didn't exist when you started this journey
- Be teaching the next generation of AI-fluent professionals
- Be looking back at this moment as the turning point in your career but all of that starts with what you do tomorrow.

Your Next Steps

You've completed the 30-day plan. Here's what comes next: This week:

- Review your workflows and optimize what's working
- Share your progress with someone who supported you
- Take the first action toward your 90-day goal
- Celebrate how far you've come

This month: Master one advanced AI technique

- Build one impressive project for your portfolio
- Help one person get started with AI

Track your time savings and calculate your ROI

This quarter:

- Develop deep expertise in AI applications for

your field

- Update your resume and LinkedIn to showcase your AI skills Pursue one opportunity that your AI skills make possible
- Reflect on your transformation and set new goals This year: Become known as someone who knows how to leverage AI
- Achieve measurable career advancement because of your skills Build a body of work that demonstrates your capabilities
- Pay it forward by teaching others what you've learned The path is clear. You have the skills. You have the plan. You have the momentum. All you have to do is keep going.

A Final Word: Adopt AI and Thrive

This book started with a stark message: Adopt AI or get replaced. That was true. The world is changing, and people who resist that change will be left behind. But here's what I want you to remember: This isn't just about survival. It's about thriving. AI isn't a threat to your career—it's the biggest opportunity you'll have in your lifetime to:

- Work smarter and reclaim your time
- Amplify your capabilities and do your best work
- Create value that wasn't possible before
- Build a career that's fulfilling, secure, and

future-proof You're not learning AI because you're afraid of being replaced. You're learning AI because you're excited about what becomes possible when you master these tools. You're not adapting out of fear. You're adapting out of ambition. And that makes all the difference.

You're Ready

You have everything you need:

- The tools are set up
- The skills are developed
- The workflows are built
- The plan is clear
- The momentum is real

The only question left is: What will you do with it? Will you let this book sit on your shelf while you go back to your old ways? Or will you take what you've learned and build something extraordinary? I think I know the answer. You didn't read this far, complete 30 days of action, and transform your capabilities just to stop now. You're not that person anymore. You're someone who adapts. Someone who learns. Someone who takes action. Someone who thrives in change instead of fearing it. You're someone who's ready for the future—because you're building it. So, go. Use what you've learned. Create something amazing. Save time. Make money. Advance your career. Help others. Build the life you want. And when you look back at this moment years from now, you'll remember it as the day everything changed. The day you stopped worrying about AI replacing you and started using AI to become irreplaceable. The day you stopped reading about the future and started creating it. The day you became the person you were always capable of being. Welcome to your AI-powered future.

Now go build it.

Conclusion: You're Ready

You just finished eight chapters that most people will never read. Not because those people are less intelligent or less motivated -- but because they are waiting. Waiting for the right moment. Waiting until they feel ready.

You did not wait. And that already puts you ahead.

You did not just read a book about artificial intelligence. You completed a curriculum. You learned what AI is and how it works. You identified the tools that matter. You developed a framework for prompting that most people never discover. And you now have a 30-day action plan that will carry you from reader to practitioner.

The only thing standing between you and your transformation is action.

Here is what to do right now:

- Open ChatGPT and complete Day 1 of the 30-day plan.
- Share what you have learned with one person who could benefit from it.
- Update your LinkedIn profile to reflect your new AI skills.
- Set a calendar reminder for 30 days from now to review your progress.

"The future belongs to those who adapt. You have everything you need. Go build the future you want. It starts today."

About the Author

Ayush Sharma

Author & AI Educator

www.victorusai.com

Ayush Sharma is an author, entrepreneur, and AI educator with a strong foundation in Computer Science, specializing in Artificial Intelligence. He is further advancing his expertise in Generative AI through studies at the Indian Institute of Technology Patna.

Driven by a passion for technology and real-world impact, Ayush focuses on helping individuals understand and apply artificial intelligence in practical ways. His work is centered on empowering students, professionals, and entrepreneurs to leverage AI for career growth, innovation, and business transformation.

With a multidisciplinary background spanning technology, business strategy, and content creation, Ayush works at the intersection of emerging technology and human performance. He has guided students, freelancers, corporate professionals, and career changers in applying AI tools effectively in their everyday professional lives.

Ayush's approach is intentionally non-technical. He believes the greatest barrier to AI adoption is not capability—but confidence. His work focuses on simplifying complex technologies, building practical skills, and delivering real, measurable outcomes.

He drives digital education initiatives and is actively engaged in shaping discussions on the future of work, AI literacy, and career development in an era defined by automation.

Adopt AI or Get Replaced is his debut book. It reflects not only his deep understanding of AI tools but also his strong belief that every individual—regardless of background, age, or technical expertise—has the ability to adapt, grow, and thrive in the era of artificial intelligence.

Connect with Ayush at **www.victorusai.com** or follow him on LinkedIn for insights on AI, productivity, and the future of work.

Words to Carry Forward

"The future belongs to those who learn more skills and combine them in creative ways."

-- Robert Greene

"In the middle of difficulty lies opportunity."

-- Albert Einstein

"You don't have to be great to start, but you have to start to be great."

-- Zig Ziglar

"The only way to do great work is to love what you do -- and to keep learning, keep adapting, keep growing."

-- Ayush Sharma

Thank you for reading Adopt AI or Get Replaced.

The future is yours to build.

www.victorusai.com

www.ingramcontent.com/pod-product-compliance
Lightning Source LLC
LaVergne TN
LVHW090316210926
848480LV00001B/265
* 9 7 9 8 9 0 5 8 4 4 1 0 2 *